— The History of the First Thirty Years —

LOOKING BACK

At Gardner Lake, Kansas

The epic struggle to complete the largest WPA Project in Johnson County and the joy and tragedy that followed

Amy Heaven

Copyright © 2022 by Amy Heaven

All rights reserved.

No portion of this book may be reproduced in any form without written permission from the publisher or author, except as permitted by U.S. copyright law.

Cover design and interior layout by Mike Fontecchio, Faith & Family Publications.

ISBN: 979-8-9871389-1-5

Printed in the United States of America

DEDICATION

This book is dedicated to the men of the Gardner Lake Corporation, who had the vision and fortitude to tackle the mammoth task of building a lake against all odds. And to the women who supported them.

And to the forgotten men who put their shoulders to the shovels as their last means of survival.

And last, but certainly not least, Pat and Bud Heaven.

I was asked "which of all the Lake cabins did you admire the most," and really, I couldn't say. I would see one and think it darling, and the next one had such attractive features, in fact, each and every one has a distinction all its own, to fit each individual. As a wife would say to her husband,

> *Please.*
> *Build me a house*
> *On Gardner Lake.*
> *Pluck down a star*
> *For its window bar.*
> *Toss in a dream.*
> *To jewel the hearth;*
> *But sink its base*
> *In the good brown earth.*

Mrs. John T. (Frances) Patty
Lake Road 13
The Gardner Gazette
August 24, 1942

I wondered what Henry Thoreau saw in Walden Pond that Gardner Lake lacks. Yes, life was good and the world at peace at Gardner Lake. Even heavy human problems should not be too difficult to settle in such calm surroundings.

The Gardner News
July 10, 1958

Contents

Dedication iii
Foreword viii
Prologue 1

PART I
The Gardner State Lake

Chapter 1: The Village of Gardner 4

Chapter 2: The Gardner State Lake 10
    Emory Fulton Alexander. 11
    The Original Cornerstone Park 13

Chapter 3: The Gardner Lake Corporation 14
    Howard C. Bigelow, Treasurer 20

Chapter 4: Transient Camp 9 21
    Vernon M. "Jack" Chesbro 25
    Vernon "Sonny" Chesbro 27
    The First Christmas at TC9 in 1934 30
    Westminster Hall in the 1930's. 32
    Irene Eastland Peer 35
    The Camp Laundry 37

Chapter 5: KERC Liquidation Leaves Project in Financial Limbo. . . . 39

Chapter 6: Work Continues at the Gardner State Lake 41
    Howard's Agony 42
    The Last Crossing of 159th Street 47
    The Caretaker's House 56
    Huts on the Move 62

PART II
The Gardner Lake Resort Years
1938-1970

Chapter 7: Ordinance 518 – Laying Down the Law 64
Chapter 8: Opening Day for Fishing Finally Arrives 68
    The Story of Fishburger 69
Chapter 9: The Public Beach 72
    When The Lake was Finally Full 74
    A Magnificent Structure 81
Chapter 10: Boat Rentals 82
Chapter 11: Gardner Lake Resort 84
Chapter 12: Gardner Lake Resort Clubhouse 86
    Raid at Gardner Lake Resort 90
    Children Die in Fire on Lake Road 5 93
Chapter 13: Keeping the Peace 98
    Gardner Lake Claims Its First Life 104
Chapter 14: The Precarious Relationship with ONAS 106
    A Slippery Situation Between Navy and Lake 112
Chapter 15: Harvesting the Lake 113
    Chig's Water War 118

PART III
The First Eighteen Years

Chapter 16: The First Families 122
    "Haderway" and "Dunwanderin" 124
Chapter 17: Fun Facts, Fables and Legends 132
Chapter 18: The Covenants 138

Epilogue: It's All in The Chase! 141
Partial Index of Gardner Lake WPA Workers: The Gardner Gazette . . . 145
    Monument to a Friendship 148
Acknowledgments 151
Bibliography 153
Index 159
About the Author 163

FOREWORD

It is an honor to introduce Amy Heaven and her work to this readership. A comprehensive history of Gardner Lake is much needed and long overdue. On the following pages, she presents a thoughtful, accurate and well-researched work of the first 30 years and beyond.

I originally met Amy back in the late 1980s, while serving as president of the Gardner Lake Association. She had contacted me about assessing a run-down historic house in Belton, MO. She was living in Olathe at the time, working in aircraft sales for Kansas City Aviation Center. Our mutual interests, that I knew of, were pretty much focused on preserving and restoring historic property. Her credibility in this area includes a robust inventory of restored historic gems during her time as a city official and resident of Lexington, Missouri. Little did I know that we would reconnect over the years and ultimately she would land at Gardner Lake, and I would move to fulfill a long career at the University of Iowa. We share a common passion for Gardner Lake, each having devoted a portion of our lives to its betterment. For each of us, the lake represents a place of civic challenge and near-idyllic enchantment at a critical point in our respective lives.

Beginning in 1975, I spent all of my 20s and much of my 30s living at the lake. Back then, our telephone service consisted of a 4-party line, which in my case included a family with teenagers and the local weekly news correspondent to *The Gardner News*. It was frequent to pick up the phone to make a call only to hear a fully-engaged conversation already happening on the other end. Early in my residency, I was invited to attend the meetings of the Gardner Lake Association. After a few meetings, I was nominated and elected to the board of directors, as director of Civil Defense. The main responsibility was carrying the key to the lake siren and letting the county know if the warning system did not go off during a test or emergency situation.

How well I remember the great tornado of May 4, 1977, which originated near Baldwin in the early evening. The atmosphere was heavy much of the day and numerous twisters were breaking out in Eastern Kansas and over to Sedalia, MO. The tornado was well-predicted, with pre-coverage on local stations, which was attributed to saving many lives. The tornado, later rated as an F-4, stayed on the ground from Edgerton, across the north end of Gardner Lake, and wound its way through the rural countryside to Olathe. As it approached the west side of the lake, soft-ball sized hail stones crashed to the ground and into the lake. My wife and neighbors having already taken cover in the next-door basement, I waited until the last possible second and saw the large funnel jump the road north of the golf course, skirting that end of the lake. Once immediately passed through, several of us watched the tall, ominous and dark funnel wind its way toward Olathe. The next day, there was a Lincoln Continental Mark IV from Douglas County that was discovered in a farm field just northeast of the lake.

Within this history of the lake, Amy points out that Herbert Hoover's Depression-era policies and the Dust Bowl Days of the Midwest set the stage for new programs that would beget many local, state and national projects. Franklin Roosevelt's New Deal politics, Civilian Conservation Corps (CCC), Workers Progress Administration (WPA) and others were aimed at providing jobs and economic relief during one of the most depressed economies in our history. Gardner was an active part of benefiting from this national effort. Gardner Lake is an historic treasure resulting from this national initiative.

One of the main protagonists of the Gardner Lake story was Emory F. Alexander, a Gardner druggist. In 1933 he was appointed by the beloved Governor Alf Landon as County Loan Chairman for Johnson County "for the purpose of arranging for farm loans for farmers in danger of losing their properties." It

Looking Back

is likely this and some other responsibilities he took on that earned him the appointment of Director of Personnel for the WPA in Topeka, then later District Director for the WPA. He was well-known and respected from Emporia to Kansas City, and especially in Olathe and Gardner. He was the main driver of the lake construction. This backdrop helps build the connections of those men and motivations around the Gardner Lake project.

In this work, Amy has captured some of the changing social pastimes in how Gardner Lake was adapted as a resort during the mid-20th Century. With the large recreation and mess hall building left over from construction worker housing, or Transient Camp #9, a ready-made entertainment venue was refitted many times to serve diverse purposes from 1940–1962. A constantly changing line of operators was creative and resourceful in adapting the facilities to the latest social amusement and fads of the times. From clubhouse, dinner and dance hall with live band and orchestras to roller skating rink and Lakeside Country Club, there were as many promoters and operators as there were uses for the resort facility. When the hall burned down, the entertainment setting came to an abrupt end, and the lake settled into the quiet and more private lakeside neighborhood that we have come to know.

The Gardner Lake Association as it operates today, initially organized at the picnic grounds by Lake Road No 10, August 11, 1957 and formally incorporated April 14, 1960. There has been a very long list of dedicated directors, lake road representatives and volunteers over the years, who took seriously the early mission: "to bring the residential owners of lots on Gardner Lake together for mutual helpfulness and united action on measures conducive to their common welfare." I could opine about the character and attitudes of each of these community servants during my time at the lake. We came together often for association meetings, spring and fall clean-up days, the annual picnic, and special initiatives such as dredging, water use, land use, the sewer proposal, all of which affected the "common welfare" of residents. My greatest personal pride during that time was the proposal, planning and construction of the substantial bridge that replaced the low-water crossing over the south end of the lake. After losing one of our local residents in a torrent, we rallied local, county and state government around the vision of a safe, solid and sturdy bridge. It took from the fall of 1985 through 1988 to see that dream of "a full concrete bridge with road

FOREWORD

surface six feet above the high-water level" to come to completion. Today's lake association continues to promote similarly beneficial interests.

Running between the lines of this history, water is the throughput for the entire story. Beginning with the lake construction project, water brought various local, regional and state players together to make the lake a reality. Anyone who has lived on Gardner Lake for any duration knows that the cyclical patterns of wet and dry years are always at play. The basin on the south end can be a barometer of the last couple year's-worth of weather, sometimes with docks resting on a dry bottom. When I lived at the lake, I was fortunate to have many opportunities to chat with the Bray brothers, Ralph and Don, who shared so many stories of their lives there before the lake was built. Sometimes they had to dig holes in the dry creek bed just to puddle enough water for the thirsty livestock. They often upended large catfish buried deep under the bone-dry creek, where there was still some thick mud and enough moisture for the fish to hibernate until the precious waters returned. When lake construction started, there was not sufficient water for domestic needs of the workers. Many dry wells were dug before finding a reliable supply.

Amy's interest and stewardship of Gardner Lake carries far beyond the fascinating history she has laid out. She has taken up the critical task of protecting and preserving this water resource for future generations. Much as with the Dustbowl days of the 1930s, we have a looming water crisis affecting the quality and quantity of drinking water. The situation today is worse and the stakes are higher. Primary aquifers have been over-pumped. Regions of the West and even in the Midwest are experiencing severe shortages of water. Major reservoirs built back in the 1930s are drying up due to overuse and climate and weather pattern changes. Farm runoff has affected the quality of water throughout the Midwest and all the way down the great Mississippi and into the Gulf of Mexico. The present generation is at the tipping point of expending its usable but unsustainable water sources in many parts of the world, partly due to exponential population growth and largely due to human practices and impact on our environment. Local reservoirs of quality water, large and small, such as Gardner Lake, should be viewed as highly-valued resources and worthy of greater protection, investment and preserved in more sustainable ways.

LOOKING BACK

My time at Gardner Lake was soothing to the soul. It was a period of personal growth, friendships never-forgotten and civic engagement. Amy's research and reminiscences, especially familiar names, personal interviews and residents' stories, brought back many fond memories of relaxing days gone-by on Gardner Lake. In this aspect, we can all thank dedicated keepers of the past, like Amy, who take time to research, compile and share our local history.

Gardner Lake, its history, past, present and future have become a burning passion for Amy Heaven. While she's had many causes to champion in her life, she says "Now I'm just working on saving a lake. Why not? 'Just another dragon to slay. Bring it on."

Dave Jackson is a retired facilities director from the University of Iowa, former president of Gardner Lake Association and Friends of Johnson County Museums. He is current president of Prairie Mutual Insurance Association, Keota, Iowa and English Valleys History Center, North English, Iowa. He can be reached at dbjiowa@netins.net

PROLOGUE
1914 – 1929

Documenting the events leading up to the Great Depression and the "Dirty Thirties" would take volumes. Although it is thought of as a national situation, the issues were certainly globally rooted in "the war to end all wars," and a destabilized Europe, Asia, Africa, and ultimately, the world.

Stateside, the era was symbolized by failed banks, closed businesses, soup lines and "Hoovervilles." Americans think of the beginning as Black Thursday on October 29, 1929, with the events on Wall Street. But for the Midwest, the problems manifested with an agricultural depression realized more than a decade earlier.

Kansas felt the world's demand for grain as foreign farmers went to war in 1914. New mechanized farming techniques fueled a regional land rush that nearly decimated the great Kansas prairie and its native tallgrasses. Debt-free family farms were mortgaged to buy tractors and additional acreage. Without the need for draft animals, undisturbed pasture went under the plow as well.

Even in this area, farmers removed all the trees from their homesteads to facilitate a higher yield. These alterations to the landscape ultimately wreaked havoc on the local environment.

With the conclusion of the war in 1919, and the gradual recovery of our neighbors abroad, demands tapered and supplies stockpiled causing plummeting commodities values and sagging profits. To make ends meet, more planting was done, thus fueling a vicious cycle.

Then came the worst drought in recorded American history. Theories state that the new farming practices caused the drought with field runoff occurring where grasses previously served to capture the moisture. The fact is that the ambitious farming practices exacerbated a desperate situation as tons of topsoil blew away, livestock perished, and inhabitants fled.

What followed were fundamental changes to federal and local governments in an effort to save the growing number of unemployed, financially devastated citizens and destitute immigrants. Unprecedented programs like FDR's *New Deal* forever changed the complexion of government, and ultimately our landscape, quite literally.

Rural Gardner Boy in March, 1938.
This shoeless young boy was a symbol of poverty with his worn, grubby overalls and a frayed coat with a safety-pin closer. He was probably cold and hungry. Sadly, he was typical of the human condition during the American Depression. (Photo courtesy of the Gardner Historical Museum)

PART I
THE GARDNER STATE LAKE

Chapter 1
THE VILLAGE OF GARDNER

The village of Gardner, established in 1857, originated at a point where the Santa Fe Trail and the Oregon and California trails diverged towards their respective destinations. Early references to Gardner described the settlement as a small trading post at the fork of three trails. In one week of May 1860, sources reported that 700 prairie schooners passed through Gardner. Running east and west through town, Main Street became the departure corridor from the popular Lone Elm campgrounds, several miles east of town where pioneers, like the trails, diverged from their former existences. This rich heritage is still embraced by the citizens today and is a source of great pride.

The village of Gardner was named for Massachusetts's governor, Henry Gardner, during a time when New Englanders were migrating west to stem the spread of slavery. The Kansas-Nebraska Act of 1854 provided a means of organizing the states of Kansas, Nebraska, Montana, and the Dakotas, for admittance into the union. However, the controversial instrument also left open the possibility that they may be admitted as slave states. These antebellum events sparked the bitter fighting along the Missouri and Kansas state lines that preceded and remained through the American Civil War. Gardner's geographic location placed it in a very vulnerable position as the abolitionist Red Legs, or Jayhawkers fought the pro-slavery Bushwhackers or

The Village of Gardner

Guerrillas. Consequently, Gardner was in Quantrill's path on his infamous raid of Lawrence and was looted by the notorious bandits, or freedom fighters, depending on one's perspective, on October 22, 1861. This is believed to be the first town in Johnson County, and possibly the state, to be raided by Confederate Bushwhackers.

The Pony Express ran down the Santa Fe Trail through Gardner beginning in 1860 but was replace by the railroad that carried mail from the town's depot in 1871.

At the time, the brushy and rolling land that is now under Gardner Lake was owned by two peaceful farmers from the Shawnee tribe of native Americans, namely Lazarus Flint and his son, James Turkeyfoot. A treaty between the tribe and the United States provided each Shawnee family member 200 acres of land. Flint, with wife Louisa and daughter Mary Jane, acquired 600 acres that encompassed the land at the north end of the lake, while Turkeyfoot owned the acreage at the south end. Flint eventually sold his acreage for $900 and left this area in 1869.

Fast forward to the 1930s, and Gardner was approaching a population of almost 500 citizens. The basis of commerce was agrarian by then. They were primarily family-centric, church-going Christians with conservative ideals, who overwhelmingly, voted Republican. The installation of progressive liberal president-elect Franklin Delano Roosevelt in March 1933 was looked upon with dread and suspicion. However, that inauguration propelled the completion of the Gardner State Lake after federal funding under Herbert Hoover fell short of the goal.

Dr. A.S. Reece, in his manuscript "Socialized Medicine at The Grass Roots" makes this observation about the town in 1930:

LOOKING BACK

"The outward appearance of the town itself showed no evidence of the depression. The people were industrious, honest, many of them retired farmers, proud of their tree-lined streets, beautiful flower gardens, and even their vegetable gardens. Main Street was extra wide and had once been a part of the old Santa Fe Trail. It still had remnants of the horse and buggy days for along the concrete walks a few hitching posts still stood and on a Saturday afternoon a wagon and team, yes occasionally even a buggy, would

Brick Block, Main Street Gardner.
This real picture postcard was taken in the decade prior to 1920. (Photo from the author's collection)

The Village of Gardner

be found hitched to one of these posts. In the middle of the block, where people would frequently run into it, was an old-fashioned pump where the old-time department store (that sold everything), the hardware store, the drug store, the harness shop, yes, harness shop, still drew buckets of water for use in their stores and shops. There was the remnant of another larger well right in the center of the street on the main corner."

Looking Back

Trails attract settlements. To facilitate the growing settlements, those trails grew into roads. With the growth of the towns, highways were needed to link the cities. In Gardner's case, the Santa Fe Trail became Main Street, and eventually Highway 56. The town, still too far from Kansas City to be considered a suburb, had primary access to the big city via Highway 50, which engulfed much of the trail northeast of Gardner. A shopping trip to Kansas City was still so extraordinary that the news of such would appear on the front page of *The Gardner Gazette*, the local newspaper published between 1889 and 1942 from offices on Main Street. In addition, commerce of any kind, due to the present economic emergency, was curtailed so drastically by the shortage of currency and the loss of income, that most of the trading in town was done by bartering. Dr. Reece, the local physician who transformed medicine in Gardner, complained in his manuscript that he couldn't pay his rent with chickens and hams. As a result of bartering, much of the labor needed to build his hospital, the first in Johnson County, came from trading work for health care. The materials were mostly recycled.

During this bleak period which lasted the entire decade of 1930, *The Gardner Gazette* had more ads for close out sales and public auctions than display ads for the local mercantile. Groceries stores, such as Lasley's (phone 166), struggled along, with only an occasional farm wife, wearing a flour sack calico dress, dropping in for a meager purchase of a necessity. The two hardware stores in town, Young's and H.M. Terrell's, the latter offering incubators and vacuum cleaners, struggled as well. On the other side of the street was Stanley Furniture and Undertaking, an unlikely combination of services that stem from the tradition of the furniture maker also being casket manufacturers. Gardner also boasted two drugstores. Local pharmacist E. E. Armstrong had his shingle on Main Street as did E. F. Alexander, whom Armstrong had mentored into the business.

The Village of Gardner

The business that dominated Gardner's Main Street in the 1930's was Bigelow-Foster Mercantile, a general store that grew into a department store and dominated the north side of Main Street for decades. Like all the downtown merchants, they had tightened their belt against strangled sales.

The largest employer in town was Cramer Chemical, located on Warren Street, who created, patented, and manufactured creams and salves for sport injuries. The brainchild of influential brothers, Chuck and Frank Cramer, their business received national recognition on the college athletic circuit. During the 1930's, they employed as many as seventy-five citizens, defying the economic situation while meeting a demand caused by an appetite for cheap entertainment.

Hungry for diversion, entertainment at the time consisted of bridge squares, picnics, and an occasional picture show, either silent or 'talkee,' being projected at the Westminster Hall, the community center next to the Presbyterian Church.

Fraternal organizations also presented options for commiserating fellowship through the Free Masons, Odd Fellows, and The Grange, who were the most prevalent. The women did their philanthropic duties at the auxiliaries to those organizations such as the Athenas, Order of the Eastern Star, and the Rebekahs.

Attending church was an important aspect of life during these hard times in Gardner, and local congregations did notable philanthropic work. Several congregations were represented in Gardner including the Presbyterians, Methodist, Baptist, Catholic, and the Church of Christ. Given the bleak circumstances of the 1930s, one would need a strong faith to endure the depressing daily news.

Once a busy and thriving town, Gardner was then quiet, hot, and dusty with an occasional car, truck, or farm wagon moving down Main Street. The nation's commerce had ground to a halt and the citizens were desperate for a solution.

Chapter 2
THE GARDNER STATE LAKE

The Construction Years 1934-1939

In 1934, the United States was in the clutches of what was to become known as the "Great American Depression." The Midwest had been in an agricultural depression in the previous decade that was being fueled by record droughts, bank failures, and the shortage of legal tender. The Farmers State Bank was compelled to print "script" for lack of currency. Gardner, a farming town with a population of roughly 500, was surviving better than most as citizens bartered with commodities from their gardens.

Progressive President Franklin D. Roosevelt was inaugurated for the first time the previous year and implemented broad and sweeping experiments to curb the national situation. He was not necessarily popular in this local Republican stronghold in Johnson County, except with a handful of Democrats who struggled for a toehold in local politics. Gardner druggist Emory F. Alexander was one of those men. Influential, Alexander won the confidence of many citizens who supported him in his tireless effort to secure government funding for farm improvements. He already successfully facilitated the construction of farm ponds to bring relief to the drought-stricken area. One of those ponds was on his farm property on 135th Street between Gardner Road and Homestead.

Emory Fulton Alexander

The Gardner Lake project was clearly the dream-child of E. F. Alexander. In 1933, while the Midwest was in the grips of a destructive and life-threatening drought, Alexander envisioned a watery oasis for Gardner. It was a project that would not only improve lives, but actually save those destitute and homeless men affected by the economic hardships of the Great Depression. The very existence of the lake is attributed to his forward thinking, tireless efforts and considerable influence.

At the time of the Gardner Lake campaign, he was described in Dr. A. S. Reece's manuscript, *Socialized Medicine at The Grass Roots,* as a slightly bald and somewhat heavy-set gentleman of medium height. Reece goes on to say that he had a slight Arkansas accent having claimed that he was raised in the "hillbilly region of Arkansas." Born in Lawrence County, Missouri, in 1880, Alexander may have been raised in Arkansas, but he settled in Gardner in the early '30s after a stint as a traveling salesman for a large pharmaceutical company of the day, Faxon Gallagher. Alexander purchased a farm north of Gardner where he and his wife, Lillian, settled and raised their one son, Mac.

Alexander was a staunch Democrat his entire life and served many years as the chairman of the Johnson County Democratic Committee. He promoted his party and candidates in a town that was overwhelmingly Republican. Politics was a favorite topic of conversation, and his new drugstore on Main Street near Elm became the center point for such discussions. A natural gathering place, Alexander's drugstore had a soda fountain with the first soft-serve ice cream in the region.

His political influence did not go unnoticed when, under Roosevelt's *New Deal*, Alexander was appointed assistant director of the Works Progress Administration (WPA) for the State of Kansas. This powerful position probably helped for a smoother transition when the Kansas Emergency Relief Committee was forced to acquiesce to the WPA's takeover of those federally funded, state-managed relief programs in October of 1935. Not unlike today, politics of the 1930's was polarizing. And, not unlike today, there was quid pro quo. Long-time Gardner native, Richard McCreary relayed a story from his youngest years when he accompanied his father, a local dairy farmer, to the camp to deliver the daily supply of milk. "Uncle Alec," as Alexander was either affectionately or sarcastically referred, approached his father and asked for a contribution to the Democrat party. When his father replied that he was a Republican, he promptly lost the milk contract. In Dr. Reece's manuscript, he alludes to this practice as being the reason he left a somewhat lucrative position as lake camp physician in mid-October of 1936. Reece discovered that he was receiving only $150 of the $200 that was allocated for the doctor's salary, and distributed by Alexander. When he confronted Alexander, he was told that $50 was being retained for pharmaceuticals that Alexander was providing.

Alexander could clearly cross the isle when it came to politics, and he was evidently beloved by both sides in Gardner where he was recognized for his contribution of several projects. However, a cynical remark would infrequently but occasionally appear in *The Gardner Gazette*. An example of this was the reference to the new car he was sporting during the financial crisis.

But all this aside, E. F. Alexander is undeniably the father of Gardner Lake. His tireless efforts remain evident in our local landscape and in many other areas in the region. He is credited with securing the construction of the Gardner Auditorium, currently the public works facility at Elm and Shawnee, and improvements to the Gardner Municipal Airport. In other counties, such as Lyon, he is credited with building more than a dozen farm ponds in that drought-ravaged area, employing dozens of relief workers.

It is also agreed that Alexander had an enormous role in the placement of the Navy Air Station just northeast of town. Virginia Johnson writes in her book "*Where the Trails Divide*" that Alexander "…had a way with him for getting things done."

Alexander's daily commute to his drugstore from his farm west of Olathe required a drive on Gardner Road. He would pass the Kill Creek basin with its beautiful rolling hills and deep gullies. It was already a weekend destination where the Martin Harrington family, with their large, 1890 farmstead situated northwest of Moonlight on 159th Street, welcomed people on their land to picnic. This area became known as "Cornerstone Park." This beautiful area was near 159th Street where it crossed Kill Creek two miles north of town. The vacant countryside endeared itself to the Gardner citizens, as it did Alexander, and the concept of a recreational lake at this location felt very natural to him.

The Original Cornerstone Park

The following is an excerpt from Sadie McIntire-Powell's memoirs of local history titled *Gardner Heritage,* published around 1995. In this piece, she recalls the area at 159th Street in the Kill Creek basin, currently submerged under the lake. The time frame would be the second decade of the 20th Century:

Kill Creek and Gardner Lake

"Where I was a little girl ninety years ago it was called Kill Creek. It was our 'Corner Stone Park'. It was a delightful place to have picnics, and many were held there; Sunday School picnics, last day of school picnics, family get togethers, just about anything of pleasure, that needed a beautiful outdoors, found a home at Kill Creek."

"It was privately owned by the Harrington's but almost all the time they shared it generously with those of us who wanted to use it. There were walnut trees galore and the Harrington's shared the nuts. I don't think we even asked permission. Each year, in the fall, dad hitched up the team to the hay rack and our whole family rode out to Kill Creek to pick up sack after sack of nuts. This took many hours and I remember getting off the hay rack when we started home, and running ahead to get to the Victor Homestead, which is now the golf course, to get a drink of water. A tin cup was always on the outside well, and I'm sure it was used many times outside of the Victor family by others as thirsty as I".

The Kill Creek Bridge.
This bridge traversed Kill Creek on Gardner Road as part of the undefined original Cornerstone Park. It was a favorite gathering place. This is believed to be the 1921 graduating class of Gardner Highschool with Harold Quaintance, Sr., on the right. This area is now submerged under Gardner Lake. (Photo courtesy of David B. Jackson archives)

Chapter 3
THE GARDNER LAKE CORPORATION

E. F. ALEXANDER HAD STRONG POLITICAL CONNECTIONS with the Democrat Party, now fully in charge of Washington. He demonstrated his access to federal relief programs by orchestrating the labor subsidized construction of several farm ponds north of Gardner. His next, and grandest objective was a large lake north of Gardner. To accomplish this huge task, it would be necessary to form a corporation to implement the project.

In August 1933, Alexander met with a hand-picked brain-trust to move the new project forward. He envisioned a 125-acre, man-made lake for both drought protection and recreation for the area. Eventually, the population galvanized behind the efforts of these men and championed what was to be the largest work-relief program in Johnson County. But the project would teeter on collapse even after the construction was well underway.

Alexander's closest colleagues on the project consisted of four influential Gardner businessmen: Robert J. Stockmyer; F. B. Lyon; E. E. Armstrong; and Howard C. Bigelow. Earlier that year, the bipartisan group began operating as a non-profit corporation known as the Gardner Lake Corporation, with Stockmyer as president. However, their charter wasn't recorded until later in May 1934. F. B. Lyon performed as vice-president, Armstrong as secretary, and Bigelow as treasurer. They issued 600 shares of stock with each of twelve

The Gardner Lake Corporation

stockholders owning fifty. The stockholders consisted, at that time, of R.J. Stockmyer, R.K. Stockmyer (R.J.'s son), E.E. Shriver, E.E. Armstrong, H.C. Bigelow, Ollie Turner, A. Bigelow, J.E. Johnson, M. R. Campbell (Wellsville), W.D. Fleming (Overland Park), Howard E. Payne (Olathe). No money changed hands. Their letterhead from November 1934 touted the board of directors, which included the original officers, and stockholders, plus L. C. Haynes of Kansas City, Kansas, and J. R. Whitlia of Edgerton. Alexander served as Chairman of the Board. The group's strategy was to secure the lake project under the state fish and game commission's authority. The construction of the Gardner State Lake could be funded with allocated federal money distributed through the Kansas Emergency Relief Committee in 1934. The plan was to borrow the funds from the state fish and game commission, purchase the land and divide it into lots. Then, they would sell the lots to repay the commission. The understanding is that they would then donate the land to the state in exchange for the labor to build the lake. The GLC received a verbal commitment from the commission, and headlines splashed across the February 21st edition of *The Gardner Gazette* reading "State Lake Assured."

Three Influential Gardner Men.
Gardner Lake Corporation members are probably gathered to discuss lake business at Farmers Bank in 1937. The men from left to right are Eric Johnson, Howard Bigelow, and Robert K. Stockmyer. Far left is Mary Griffin Ewing. (Photo courtesy of the Arnold Johnson Archives)

Robert J. Stockmyer, President

Gardner Lake Corporation

Robert J. Stockmyer was a man of action in Gardner and a venerable supporter of projects to improve the community. Born in Fort Scott, Kansas in 1876, he made the move to Gardner in 1917 at the age of 41.

Prior to coming to Gardner, Stockmyer had been a rural mail carrier on horseback. He later served as a railway mail clerk and ascended to a post office inspector in the west and Midwest regions of the United States. He moved to Kansas to become a dairy farmer and rancher on a 600-acre farm north of town. It may have been during this transition to gentleman farmer that he made the acquaintance of neighbor E. F. Alexander, who handpicked him for the position of president of the Gardner Lake Corporation.

Of all the GLC board members, he appears to have been most aligned with Alexander's enthusiasm for opportunities and the many collateral benefits. He is also the only board member, besides Alexander, who had held a position with the federal government. At age 57, he still had the energy of a much younger man.

He approached his other appointed position on the Johnson County Fair Association with equal gusto.

During lake construction, it was Stockmyer's task to secure the enormous amount of money needed to guarantee the lake's success. Eventually, when the money fell short, Stockmyer was one of the four GLC members compelled to pledge their homes to secure the necessary funding to get the lake project completed.

Stockmyer and his wife, Minnie, had four children including a young daughter that died at 11 months. There was a son name John and a daughter named Jean. Robert Kirkland, 'R. K.' was the son who held a prominent position with the Farmers Bank and also served the GLC. When the long-awaited event occurred on April 18, 1937, and the lots were assigned to individuals who had purchased the $100 tickets, R. J. Stockmyer's young granddaughter, and R. K. Stockmyer's daughter, Joan, pulled those names from a glass bowl determining the lot assignments.

The Gardner Lake Corporation

It is unknown how they knew each other, or how they interacted socially, but what is known is that they put forth a tireless effort against enormous odds and brought something together that has impacted, and will continue to impact, thousands. With hours of travel to and from Topeka, and meetings in smoky office buildings, they finally cleared the regulatory hurdles, which were considerable.

Now, the bar was quite high for them during 1934. Alexander's team was tasked with raising the money to purchase the land to be donated to the state fish and game commission for the completion of the project. Bear in mind, this was a time of total financial upheaval that cannot even be imagined by future generations. The lots would consist of fifty feet of lake front, 150 feet deep, and were priced at one hundred dollars per lot. They felt the first forty lots would sell relatively quickly, but the last sixty lots would be a challenge, even with the generous terms of ten dollars down and low monthly installments. Later, that estimate to purchase all the land, would rise to $16,000; a sum equivalent to $320,000 in 2020 money.

Frank B. Lyon, Vice President,
Gardner Lake Corporation

To have pulled together this seemingly impossible lake project, locals needed a leadership team of high-profile, high-functioning, and highly respected achievers. The task was accomplished with people like Frank B. Lyon, who was elected vice president of the Gardner Lake Corporation upon its inception in 1933.

Born in Gardner in 1871, Lyon was the most mature of the board members. At the ripe age of 17, he joined Bigelow-Foster Mercantile where he beloved for his tireless work ethic and service to the public. Lyon made a career of retailing and eventually became a partner with Bigelow until his retirement in 1949. The stored ended shortly after that, as did Lyon, who passed away in 1951.

During Lyon's active years in Gardner, he was the treasurer for the Johnson County Republican Party, and his name appears on the roster of most of the town's fraternal organizations, including the Gardner Lodge No. 65 AF & AM where he was eventually elected as lodge master. He also belonged to the Order of the Eastern Star and Modern Woodmen of the World. He was an active member of the Gardner Presbyterian Church, and a tireless volunteer. Alex G. Powers, in his book, *A History of Gardner Masonic Lodge No.65*. published in 2018, says this about the man: "This book would not have been possible if it were not for the lodge records that I depended upon so heavily for the information presented here. We have those lodge records today because of the courageous actions of one man, Brother Frank B. Lyon. During the tragic lodge fire in 1906, all was lost except for the lodge records, as Brother Lyon ran into the burning building to save them. Gardner Lodge meant a lot to Frank Lyon. I don't know too many people that would run into a building engulfed in flames over some record books. If he had not taken the action that he did, a book of this extent would not be possible."

In early March, the GLC learned from Topeka that they would be required to provide the materials for the project in addition to the land. Those additional expenses were estimated at $5,600. Uncertain how they were going to sell the original goal of 100 lots in the current economy, they would now need to sell another forty or fifty. Seeing the economic benefit of tourism in this area, the chamber of commerce in Olathe stepped up to commit to selling twenty-five lots. Kansas City, Kansas, did as well. All in all, they had eighteen months to sell 150 lots.

Eldon E. Armstrong, Secretary
Gardner Lake Corporation

One of the eldest members of the Gardner Lake Corporation, at 56 years of age, was Eldon E. Armstrong. Armstrong, like Bigelow, was deeply rooted in Gardner with his grandparents being among the original settlers in 1860. To Armstrong fell the duties of corporate secretary.

A local druggist, Armstrong was credited with mentoring E. F. Alexander into the drugstore business. Their warm relationship dates back to the time that Alexander was "drumming" pharmaceuticals for Faxon Gallagher and calling on Armstrong while making his rounds.

Armstrong's profile in town was that of a man highly respected and influential. He was a credit to the board and remembered fondly by all.

The GLC received a blow when the Kansas Supreme Court ruled that it was unconstitutional for the state fish and game commission to make a loan of federal relief funds for the purpose of purchasing the necessary land for the lake basin. Now, the GLC would be required to sell 150 *theoretical* lake lots for one hundred dollars each on land the GLC didn't own, to raise the necessary funds for the purchase of that same land. *The Olathe Mirror* announced on March 8, 1934, that "The death knell was sounded to the hopes of the Gardner Lake".

R. K. Stockmyer took the lead on the sale of lots aided by the newspaper and most of the area merchants. He went so far as to give *Kansas City Star* reporter, Bill Moore, a future lot if he would write often and favorably about the project. After tireless efforts to raise the enormous sum of money, they fell short. Stockmyer was one of four board members who pledged his home to cover the balance. However, the challenge of raising that money would be matched only by the agony of acquiring the land and the sixteen deeds necessary to get the dam built and flood the lake basin. This task fell squarely, and hard, on Howard Bigelow. Had the GLC failed, board members would have lost their homes and suffered the consequences of defaulting on numerous real estate contracts. Hours of struggle would have been for not, and the logistics of returning money raised, if that were even possible, would have been monstrous. The GLC board of directors made a narrow escape of this probable outcome on at least two occasions.

Howard C. Bigelow, Treasurer

Gardner Lake Corporation

A lifelong citizen of Gardner, Howard Bigelow was 45 years of age in 1934 and was serving as a cashier at Farmers Bank. He was the fair-haired son of retailer Art Bigelow, sporting wire rim glasses and seldom seen without a cigar. As treasurer of the GLC, it was his enormous responsibility to secure the property needed for the lake basin and the surrounding parks, without any funds.

Bigelow must not have been a stranger to hard work. He helped to establish the Farmers Bank in 1910 and served as managing officer until his retirement in 1953. He then continued as Chairman of the Board until January 1, 1969. He also served as president of the Kansas Bankers Association from 1942-1943. He was very proud of the fact that, during the depression, his bank always found a way for a property owner to avoid foreclosure. His only hiatus from banking was to proudly serve his country as First Lieutenant in World War I.

Prior to his banking career, he attended the University of Kansas where he served as president of the Sigma Nu fraternity. Obviously liked and trusted, he was elected mayor of Gardner in 1919 at the age of 30, and served in that capacity until 1923.

Howard Bigelow passed away on February 13, 1969 and was laid to rest at the Gardner Cemetery. A glowing resolution honoring him was adopted by the Kansas Bankers Association in May of that year.

Chapter 4
TRANSIENT CAMP 9

What occurred in the summer of 1934 was a galvanizing of Gardner citizens, local farmers, and urban neighbors in an unprecedented display of support for the Gardner Lake Corporation and the emerging lake project. During this pivotal year, the landscape north of Gardner began to change dramatically, although often tentatively and precariously.

The ensuing project required the construction of a work camp to house, feed, clothe, and care for hundreds of men. Funding for this was provided by the Kansas Emergency Relief Committee implementing federal money. Labor was supplied by the transient services arm of the Federal Emergency Relief Agency.

The allocated funds needed to feed dozens, then hundreds of relief workers comprised of destitute, unattached men from all vocations, with a large number of mature and even aging WWI veterans. They were mostly from Kansas City and Topeka, but many were just drifters picked up at railroad junctions. Some stayed for just a few days, but many stayed for years being bound there by only the promise of a few dollars a week, plus food, and board, an improvement over their former situation. Initially, these workers were viewed with suspicion or considered lazy and shiftless. But that perception was altered by newspaper reviews that touted the quality of the men, townhall meetings that outlined the objective and progress, and open houses at the camp for public familiarization.

Work began in April 1934 with the necessary surveys to determine the shorelines and runoff potential. The following month, materials began to arrive to build a modern, if not comfortable, camp to house the necessary workers forecasted to number 300. The corporation hired local contractors.

Looking Back

Area farmers rented out their teams of horses and mules to help clear the timber. The camp construction, managed by the Kansas Emergency Relief Committee, was located on the Cristler family farm, what is now Lake Road 5. It became known as Transient Camp #9.

Transient Camp 9
Built by the Kansas Emergency Relief Committee starting in 1934, TC9 served as housing for hundreds of desperate transient workers for the four years that followed. The camp was located on Lake Road 5. The property above the camp site in this photo is now submerged under Gardner Lake. (Photo courtesy of the Gardner Lake Association)

Transient Camp 9

In the interim, a tent camp was established just west of that location on the John McGrath farm, and a dozen men convened to prepare the camp site to the east. The population of that camp steadily increased as word got out that there were paying jobs. The following month, twenty more men reported for duty. By late June, there were twenty-five to thirty men working on their more permanent housing. Most anticipated the camp would be ready for occupancy in mid-August.

But the planner's largest obstacle was the water supply for the camp's consumption. In the consecutive years of crippling drought, Kill Creek was reduced to a trickle and was an inadequate source for the workers' needs. Workers tried digging wells to no avail, and the supply of water was a constant issue.

It is interesting to note that the state lakes at Gardner and at Eskridge in Wabaunsee County were among the first of the transient projects for unattached men to be established in the United States, with Wabaunsee getting the earlier start. In the summer of 1934, work began on camps in Dodge City and the counties of Sedan and Howard in Kansas.

The May 23, 1934 issue of *The Gardner Gazette* heralded the arrival of big government trucks delivering supplies and equipment to "Lake Town." The following month, the Gardner Lumber Company delivered their first load of materials, and contracts were awarded to other local merchants. Gardner was transforming into a "boomtown," as described one citizen.

Sadly, the first well dug on Cristler's farm proved to be dry, and a second attempt was made. Before the project was completed, a total of six wells were dug, with only the last two capable of meeting demands.

With the grounds cleared for the camp and foundations made for the various buildings, work proceeded on the structures themselves. "A good-sized force of carpenters are on the job, being assisted by the camp workers" reported *The Gardner Gazette*, as local professionals helped. Plumbers from Wellsville directed the efforts to set up the shower house.

Looking Back

The well water was filtered near the camp through a sandy lagoon constructed at the present-day location of 15787 Gardner Place, which evidently also housed the pump to deliver it to a water tower. During an interview with Robert Stockmyer, R. J. Stockmyer's grandson, he recalled the time when his father owned that property in the late '60s. Robert was tasked with digging out the sand, which was considerable as he recalls. He was only in his early teens at the time. It made a lasting impression.

At that time, Transient Camp 9 had a newly appointed Camp Superintendent in Vernon M. "Jack" Chesbro. A native of Chautauqua County, New York, Chesbro served honorably in the World War and was discharged in 1919. Prior to his brief career with the KERC, he was wildcatting oil in Garnett, Kansas, and ran a hotel in Ottawa. But he soon moved his family to the superintendent's cabin at the camp site. When school started for his two boys, they purchased and moved to a house on Main Street in Gardner. His wife, Ferne, established herself as a social fixture in town, and his young sons, Charles and Vernon "Sonny," were adopted as mascots at the camp.

Chesbro family portrait taken during the lake construction years.
Vernon "Sonny" Chesbro stands on the left with Charles "Charlie" on the right between Jack and Ferne. (Photo courtesy of Linda Chesbro Wedman)

Vernon M. "Jack" Chesbro

Transient Camp 9 Superintendent

Few men at the camp garnered as much respect and admiration as Jack Chesbro. And it was certainly well-earned. During Chesbro's four-year tenure, *The Gardner Gazette* often waxed poetic about his capabilities, likeability and leadership skills. Chesbro, along with his wife Ferne, and their two young sons, Vernon Jr. "Sonny" and Charles, were given a hero's welcome when they moved to Gardner from Ottawa in 1934. Ferne found her niche in the social circles, and the boys made friends quickly.

Chesbro was born in 1886 in western New York State, putting him at the age of 48 when ground was broken for the camp. He served honorably in the World War and was discharged in 1919. Chesbro ended up in Ottawa, Kansas, as the manager of the National Hotel, where he met and married local resident Ferne Sowers in 1921. After the stint as a hotel manager, he started wildcatting oil in that area, according to his oldest son, Vernon Jr's memoirs. The June 24, 1933, issue of *The Iola Daily Register* states that Governor Landon appointed him as foreman at the Fegen Lake Camp, another early relief project in Woodson County. Eventually he was appointed superintendent of the Gardner State Lake Transient Camp 9. How he ended up working for the Kansas Emergency Relief Committee is unknown, but the record indicates that he was very successful in his various positions.

He wrote prolifically for *The Gardner Gazette*, adapting himself to public relations duties and was able to function with poise in social settings. Every indication suggests that while at the helm, the camp was peaceful, and the men behaved with discipline.

Chesbro was missed by "the boys" upon his transfer to the sister project at Wabaunsee Lake near Eskridge, Kansas, in 1937. Joe Jerovic, electrician at the project, was so moved by their friendship that he returned to Gardner to posthumously commemorate Chesbro in 1991 with a bell from a Santa Fe Railroad locomotive. It is mounted in a permanent monument at Cornerstone Park. Chesbro's granddaughter has a treasured, handcrafted trunk given to him, presumably, by the camp carpenter, James Edenbo. Edenbo was the 'camp wood surgeon' and was responsible for making game boards and furniture.

When the relief work projects were finally done, Chesbro took his wife and sons to Kinsley, Kansas, where they had purchased the hotel. He and Ferne divorced shortly thereafter, and Chesbro returned to his home state of New York, and she to Ottawa.

Jack Chesbro, Superintendent of Transient Camp 9
Chesbro took command of the camp in 1934 but was eventually transferred to the Lake Wabaunsee project in 1937 to the disappointment of his wards. (Photo courtesy of the Linda Chesbro Wedman family archives)

LOOKING BACK

In late August, in an effort to secure a water supply, workers dug a sixth well. With anticipated success of the sixth well, work began on a thirty-foot water tower located in the center of the camp. Between flanking rows of barracks, adjacent the water tower, a pyramid shaped stone monument stood and featured a tall flagpole. This made up the centerpiece of the mall area and greeted the men as they came and went from their quarters. The camp was an austere, dusty place and lacked any vegetation, trees or grass.

October's first two editions of *The Gardner Gazette* heralded that, "The big mess and recreation hall is about ready for occupancy." They announced a big housewarming party planned for October 19, with everyone invited and everything free of charge. This was one of several events designed to win the hearts of those Gardner citizens who were still leery of having a large force of destitute and homeless men so close to their town. But by now, one might assume that their fears would have been quelled. The stimulation of commerce to the community was certainly welcomed, and the worker's arrival to town caused no problems to date.

Vernon "Sonny" Chesbro

It's a wonderful thing when one can achieve their fondest memories during the worst chapter in our American economic history. Vernon "Sonny" Chesbro, son of Jack and Ferne Chesbro, certainly did that. Just nine years old at the time, Sonny, and his younger brother Charles, had the run of Transient Camp 9. Being the two sons of the camp superintendent had its privileges, and Sonny capitalized on them during their stay between 1934 and 1937.

In his personal memoirs, Vernon writes fondly of his friendship with the Bray boys, who lived at 28835 W. 151st Street. The Bray property backed up to the lake project, and their access to the camp was a short hike through the brush. With no phone, the boys concocted an alternate means of communication. "We had a flag system that we used to determine when we would meet to play," Chesbro later wrote.

After the Chesbros moved from the camp to the town of Gardner to facilitate the boys' schooling, Vernon became acquainted with the Cramer family and the Cramer Chemical Company, that manufactured sports medications and salves. He recalls, "On Saturdays we would go by the plant and they would let us dip into a barrel of dextrose tablets to take on a hike. These were like candy to us."

Sadly, Vernon's father was transferred to the Lake Wabaunsee project and the family moved to Topeka. But certainly, he made new friends and memories wherever he went. The *Gardner Gazette* carried news, for years after his departure, of Sonny's advancement through the Boy Scouts and eventually his wedding. He had endeared himself so.

Sonny Chesbro, along with brother Charlie, were fixtures at the camp and revered as mascots.
(Photo courtesy of Linda Chesbro Wedman)

LOOKING BACK

The big housewarming event, hosted by Jack Chesbro and the men of Transient Camp 9, was planned and executed by a social "Who's Who" of Gardner. Mrs. Earl Eyerly, the wife of a prominent grocer in town, oversaw the event planning. Wives and daughters of GLC members, stockholders and city leaders populated the sub-committees. One would imagine that each wife was probably trying to outdo the other's efforts. Consequently, the result was lavish. Supporters descended on the camp with lawn furniture, mirrors, and even Indian blankets for décor. The new buildings were resplendent with baskets of flowers and fall foliage.

Opening music was provided by a Wellsville jazz band, which was followed by short remarks from R. J. Stockmyer, President of the GLC. He introduced John Stutz, executive secretary of the Kansas Emergency Relief Committee. Stutz, a staunch Republican, fought to maintain state control of the many projects implemented by the KERC, but was forced to acquiesce when the federal WPA took over. He shared the podium with G. F. Price, superintendent of transient relief.

Later, they cleared the big floor of the hall for dancing to live music provided by an orchestra. As the big mess and recreation hall overflowed, attendees struck up card games in the hospital and other outbuildings. Elsewhere at the camp, there was square dancing.

Estimates of attendance at the Friday night event topped 2000 people, but it was hard to know for certain as citizens came and left all night. Traffic was directed by the camp workers. But clearly, over 2,000 donuts and cookies were consumed along with gallons of lemonade. All in all, the event was considered a huge success. This was the first of several celebrations to take place at Transient Camp 9 over the next four years.

As 1934 drew to a close, workers finished structures in Transient Camp 9. They took advantage of the talent living among the men. The ranks of the workers included painters, plumbers, masons, plasterers, and even a newspaper man. All in all, they completed a total of seventeen buildings at the camp. Among those buildings were ten bunk houses, or huts as they were referred, with each sleeping eight men. Photographic evidence suggests that several of these bunk houses appeared on other parts of the lake as the work progressed geographically. In dimension, they measured twenty-two feet wide by fifty-one feet long.

Four Tourists' Cabins at Gardner Lake Resort
Ten of these structures were located at Transient Camp 9. Designed as weekend rentals, they served dual purpose during the camp construction days as additional housing then left behind in the late 1930's for rental cabins. (Photo by Buford Morrison, courtesy of the Gardner Lake Association)

In addition to the huts, there was the hospital, the large recreation and mess hall with kitchen, bathhouse/lavatory, office, superintendent's residence, garage, and storeroom. The north end of the camp was dotted with thirteen smaller cabins designed to be left as tourist rentals. It is interesting to note that several of those have survived and have been incorporated, at their original locations, into contemporary homes on the north shore of Lake Road 5. Several were moved to other locations on the lake, or possibly to town. One example of these relocated cabins, still on the lake, can be seen at 16036 Gardner East Road (Lake Road 6).

Elsewhere at this time, the lake basin was transformed in anticipation of the final shoreline. The stone bridge with two arches was completed on the east road, and the existing farm ponds were adapted for eventual connection to the lake. The Harrington's farm pond is now the silt pond east of that stone bridge, and the Bray pond is the silt pond on Gardner Road East just south of 152nd Street on the northeast corner of the lake.

Of premier importance at this time, rains and snow melts filled the local wells so the water issue was finally resolved. Water from two adjoining wells located northwest of the camp was pumped into the newly completed, 1500 gallon water tank which stood thirty feet tall in the center of the camp mall. The seventy-two residents finally enjoyed their first hot showers.

The citizens of Gardner were very proud and supportive of the project and its participants, as they watched with captivated interest. The season of giving had arrived, and the locals answered the call. Grocers brought sacks with candy, peanuts, and fruits. The wife of Jack Chesbro, superintendent of the project, made popcorn balls for all.

The First Christmas at TC9 in 1934

By December of 1934, the transient camp on Lake Road 5 was a bustling place. Eight bunk houses were completed and a ninth very close. A foundation for a tenth bunk house was underway. A recreation hall was ready, as was a well-equipped hospital. A big kitchen was done with eleven ranges, sinks, an ice box and other fixtures. This complex, designed to house indigent, unattached males, became Johnson County's largest WPA project during the hard times of the Great Depression.

The population of the camp swelled to 72 by that time but would soon number more than 250 as plans were made to begin the construction of the dam the following month. These men, a vast number of which were WWI veterans, were paid just a few dollars a week to do the back-breaking work that is so easily accomplished today with large machinery.

The citizens of Gardner were very proud and supportive of the project and its participants as they watched with great interest. Locals answered the call of the season of giving. Grocers brought sacks with candy, peanuts and fruits. Ferne Chesbro, wife of the project's superintendent, made popcorn balls for all. After all, it was Christmas and some of these men would not be home for months and years as they cycled in and out from Kansas City, Topeka and surrounding areas.

Answering the Dinner Bell
Transient workers file into the big camp mess hall where they were fed a hot meal on large, placer mining pans. The cost of feeding, housing and clothing each man was 18 cents a day. The dining hall, which survived the camp days to become the Gardner Lake Resort clubhouse, was the focal point of camp activities. (Photo courtesy of the Olathe Public Library)

In early 1935, amenities at the camp now included a tobacco and candy counter in the rec/mess building. It was run as a separate enterprise to support and fund the appointments at the rec center, which now included a donated piano, game boards, and reading materials. Federal funds only covered the basic maintenance of the men, which was calculated at eighteen cents a day. Payday was a big event at the work camp as it helped workers acquire those few amenities. R. K. Stockmyer, a GLC board member and son of corporation president R. J. Stockmyer, was an assistant cashier at Farmers Bank. He was tasked with those much-anticipated events. Stockmyer was interviewed by John Nichols in a thesis that Nichols wrote in 1996 and said, "He remembers traveling out to the construction site wearing a double pocket carpenter's apron. In one pocket were the one-dollar bills and five dollar bills, and the change was in another. Workers would trade a work receipt with their name printed on it for the month's wage."

LOOKING BACK

In early February of 1935, a camp basketball team emerged. They played other local teams, such as the Gardner All-Stars, at the Westminster Hall located in town. Before the camp was finally closed in 1939, the camp 'boys' would have basketball and softball teams, horseshoes matches, and boxing events as some of their diversions.

The following month, plans were announced for doubling the size of the camp, although this never happened. With a population of seventy-one at the camp, they were nowhere near capacity. Outside of the camp, workers planted eight acres to help feed the camp.

Westminster Hall in the 1930's

In 1915, the First Presbyterian Church on East Shawnee Street between Center and Elm Streets answered the town's need for a community center by constructing the Westminster Hall adjacent to their church to the west. It was only a Quonset hut that measured 48' wide by 90' deep, but it turned out to be the ideal gathering spot for the relatively young town. With a large, open maple floor, it was perfect for athletic events, large town meetings and dances. A stage accommodated theatrical productions and talent shows.

Westminster was a common evening destination for the boys of the camp. They either walked the mile and a half from the camp, or got a ride in one of the camp's Ford trucks. But they turned up there frequently to play basketball, roller skate or attend Vaudevillian-like productions.

In 1938, E.F. Alexander secured the Municipal Auditorium project on Elm Street near Shawnee as the next big WPA project to benefit Gardner. When it opened the following year, it replaced Westminster as the social nucleus of the town. The Presbyterians sold the Westminster Hall at a public auction for $1,600 in 1944. Years later it was destroyed by fire.

Transient Camp 9

On April 3, 1935, fifteen new Ford dump trucks arrived. They were stored in a newly constructed shed near the dam. Also at that location was a blacksmith's shop and maintenance garage. They were positioned near the Kill Creek bridge on Gardner Road, an area which is now submerged off Pirate's Cove. The previous week, the camp took delivery of an elevating grader, a blade grader, and two big Caterpillar tractors. They also received a steam shovel and another big tractor. The following week, the last of the heavy equipment arrived. It included a large power shovel and dragline.

Preparatory Work at the Dam Site.
This was probably taken in early 1935. Looking east, Gardner Road is visible at the top of the picture. (Photo courtesy of the Gardner Historical Museum)

Building the Puddle Trench
Preliminary excavation was underway for the puddle trench that ran the length of the dam and formed the base of the earthen structure. The trench was then filled with a heavy clay mixture that prevented the water from undermining the structure. This photo was taken in late 1935. (Photo courtesy of the National Archives and Records Administration)

Filling the Puddle Trench
A clay mixture was deposited in the puddle trench to prevent leaking under the dam. (Photo courtesy of the Johnson County Museum)

Transient Camp 9

May of that year brought heavy, destructive rains causing considerable damage at the camp in the first week of the month. This impeded the progress of the 145 men who had reported for duty.

A massive July 4th celebration at the lake was held, reported the June 26, 1935, edition of *The Gardner Gazette*. The follow-up article on July 10 reported that the day was filled with softball games, a horseshoe pitching tournament, a tug-of-war, and lots of picnicking. The evening was especially exciting with square and round dances to a live orchestra, fireworks, and open-air "talkies."

Irene Eastland Peer

She was there. Irene remembers attending the big 4th of July celebration at Gardner Lake in 1935. At the time, she was just a young girl, but she distinctly remembers attending the event with her parents. They took a little time off from the family farm in Bonita to make the trip west to attend the highly touted event, which did not disappoint. Peer remembers the amazing display of fireworks, which ended in the brilliant illumination of the American Flag made of sparklers. It was mounted on a frame and positioned on the hill, which is now the golf course.

Peer had been a lake resident for almost 30 years. She is seen here holding a small block of wood with a limb and tiny axe. This was given her, as a girl, by Neil 'Cot' Cordell, whose trucking company handled the lake's transportation needs during the construction years. This charming object commemorated the construction of the lake and was made by camp workers during their down time.

Sadly, Irene passed from us in the Summer of 2022 after her 100th birthday. She will be missed by her friends and family.

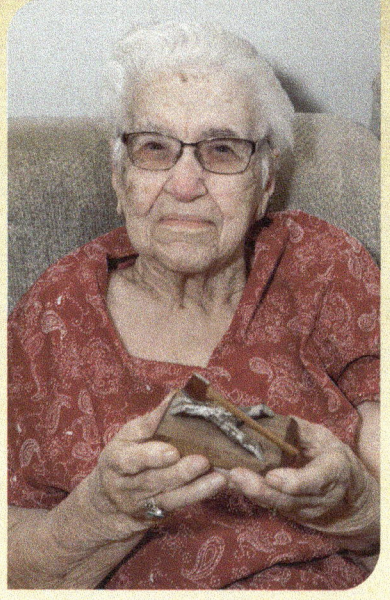

Irene Eastland Peer
Irene proudly displays the Gardner Lake memento she was given by Neil 'Cot' Cordell when she attended the July 4th, 1934, celebration at the lake project. Although a young girl at the time, she has vivid and fond memories of the occasion, especially the fireworks. (Photo courtesy of Sandy Adams, Adams ProPhoto)

LOOKING BACK

Neil 'Cot' Cordell – 1950
Neil 'Cot' Cordell owned a trucking firm in Gardner during the construction of the lake. He would use his truck to pick the workers up from camps that sprung up along the railroad tracks. He was beloved by the workers for giving them rides to and from town for evening and weekend amusement. When Cordell's brother died, the men took up a collection for flowers. The Cordell's were personal friends of Eastlands. (Photo courtesy of Alex G. Powers)

Axe and Log Souvenir
Detail of a token from the July 4, 1934, celebration at the Gardner Lake project. These were probably made by the transient workers in their spare time. (Photo courtesy of Sandy Adams, Adams ProPhoto)

Early in July, the first and only issue of *The Spillway* was published by the camp press. The newsletter consisted of fourteen pages printed front and back in the camp office, stapled together and passed out to the men of the camp. These quaint publications were done in other camps around the country and shared. It touts on the cover that Transient Camp 9 was "THE MOST HOME LIKE TRANSIENT CAMP." The society page consisted of quips such as, "'Singin' Sam" Johnson spent the weekend of June 16 in Lawrence." It continued to say, "The trip was financed by the crap shooting element of Camp Gardner."

Excerpted from *The Spillway* published July, 1935

The Camp Laundry
By MR. ANONYMOUS

In the course of my usual morning stroll last Friday, I wandered around the south side of the wash room when my ears were greeted by the whir of motors and the rhythmic song of perfectly running machinery. It instantly occurred to me that Friday is the regular wash day for the clients and here was a golden opportunity for me to acquire an insight into the workings of an up-to-date laundry. So I entered and sought out the genial superintendent of the plant, Mr. Tracy East.

"Mr. East", I began, "I know you are an extremely busy man and have not time to waste on curious idlers but I have seen a great deal of this work done by this laundry and I'm very anxious to watch the machinery in operation and to learn something of how an industrial giant runs his business. Do you mind if I watch that bundle of clothing go through the various processes that lead up to the finished product?"

"Not at all," responded Mr. East. "Only I don't like that last crack of yours about a 'finished product'. There is still a great deal of wear left in clothing after it leaves our plant."

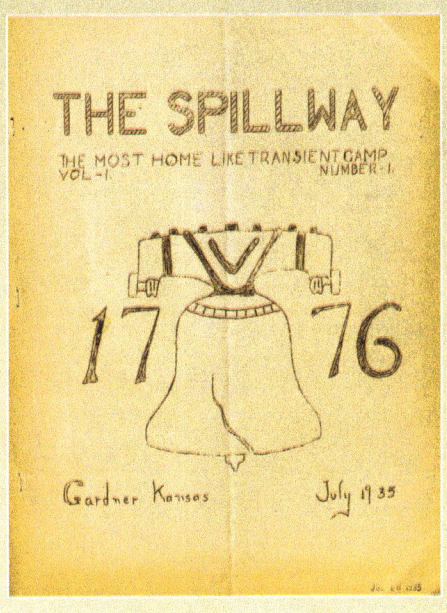

The Spillway Vol 1, Number 1
The cover of the one and only *Spillway* publication produced on site by camp workers in 1935. It was intended to be distributed among other Kansas camps as a morale booster. The project was promoted by the Kansas Emergency Relief Committee. (Courtesy of the John Stutz collection, Kenneth Spencer Research Library)

I let that pass and sat down upon a nail keg, resolving not to bother Mr. East with further questions. But when the clothing was removed from the machine to the rinsing tub, my curiosity got the better of me.

"Mr. East", I ventured, "I have often wondered how you secure your color effects in this business. Now take that undershirt, for example. I am quite certain that it was white when you put it into the machine and now its color is orchid with a slight greenish tint. How do you account for that?"

Mr. East shot me a pitying glance and replied: "The color effect is produced by a secret process of which I am the discoverer. I can tell you the formula but you won't understand it." Thereupon he launched into an explanation in highly technical language which soon convinced me that the formula was too complex for the lay mind to grasp. All I remember of it is that many different factors, such as the date, air temperature, and the number of Mexicans in Walla Walla, Washington, have to be considered.

About that time a client entered and asked for his laundry. With amazing speed and dexterity, Mr. Blankenbaker, Mr. East's first assistant, reached over and tossed the client a bundle.

"How, I inquired, "do you know that you gave that boy the right bundle?"

"We don't" chorused Messrs. East and Blankenbaker. "But that is his lookout", added Mr. East. "When we toss a client a bundle, we have discharged our obligation and if he is not satisfied to take the bundle we give him he can look for his own bundle. How far would we get if we had to stop and hunt up the right bundles for these guys?"

"Just one more question, Mr. East", "Do you regard the Working Bird Laundry in Hut 4 West seriously as a business competitor?"

A sneer crossed Mr. East's handsome countenance as he replied: "We are not afraid of the Working Bird. As long as a laundryman tries to keep one hand in a wash tub and the other on the cash register he cannot hope to be considered in a serious light. We are after "VOLUME" and spare neither time nor expense in seeking ways to improve our service. For instance, Mr. Blankenbaker has been finding it difficult to adjust his hand to the handle of our new electric iron so we are having made special for us a new handle, shaped like a plow handle of the type with which Mr. Blankenbaker is more or less familiar."

I thanked Mr. East for his courtesy and made my departure, conscious of the fact that I had spent a most profitable morning. During the month of July, I will visit the establishment of the Camp Barber and give you my impression of it in the next issue.

Chapter 5
KERC LIQUIDATION LEAVES PROJECT IN FINANCIAL LIMBO

In 1935, Franklin Roosevelt's 'New Deal' brought an influx of much-needed relief funding as the Kansas Emergency Relief Committee's (KERC) budget was exhausted. Federal funds administered by the Federal Emergency Relief Administration (FERA) flowed through the state organization. FERA was the primary relief agency during the period of 1933-35 with national distributions in excess of three billion dollars. However, FERA was never designed for operation in perpetuity, and the 1935 Congress voted to dismantle the program in deference to the Works Progress Administration (WPA). As a footnote, in 1938, the name of the program changed to Works Projects Administration in conjunction with its reorganization.

On September 5, 1935, the KERC was terminated by federal order with liquidation later that month. However, the switch-over experienced delays that left two state lake projects in the lurch that fall. Wabaunsee Lake was 14.7 percent completed and Gardner only 8 percent completed when work stopped due to the failure of funding. At Gardner, the completed work included the clearing of 130 acres of the Kill Creek basin. Six acres were prepared at the dam site including the construction of the puddle trench the length of the base, and the outlet box. Six miles of roads were graded with gravel crushed and piled for their completion. Six miles of wood fencing surrounded the stalled project. Expenditures to date at Gardner were $102,616.68, equivalent to over two million dollars in 2020 money.

E. F. Alexander steadily gained influence and recognition in Kansas and in October 1935, was promoted by Republican governor Alf Langdon to the lofting position of personnel director of the WPA for the State of Kansas. His influence must have been pivotal when the Gardner site was considered for continuation under the WPA. As a stop-gap measure, the states' KERC applied for and received an additional $300,000 while they awaited approval for their inclusion with the federal program. During the interim, the heavy equipment was serviced and stored. The men, with nowhere else to go, were limited to doing only camp maintenance in exchange for shelter and meals. During the shift, no wages were available to be paid.

"The men remaining in the camp by November 1935, represented definitely homeless, unattached, non-resident persons with no employment and for whom no state or political subdivision had legal responsibility" as stated a KERC press release on January 23, 1936. The Gardner camp became the repository of desperate men from other lake projects, too. The release continued, "It may be reasonably expected that the state will find some method in the near future by which it can complete these two lakes, since the necessary machinery, tools, and materials are now on the sites." Citizens in nearby Gardner were deeply concerned for the outcome of the project, which at the time would have resembled more of a sight of destruction.

Final approval by the WPA to continue the projects was achieved in November of 1935; however, state WPA officials had not yet bought off on reopening the projects due to the additional funding issues. The work finally resumed sometime after January 1936. During that time, 400 transient workers were housed at Wabaunsee and Gardner's camp. The workers then received raises to seventy-five dollars a month, which helped bolster morale. The condition of the camp at that time was greatly improved.

Chapter 6

WORK CONTINUES AT THE GARDNER STATE LAKE

In April 1936, work went to a twenty-four-hour schedule by running a third shift. Flood lights were installed at the dam to facilitate the night crew, with all racing the clock to complete the project before another funding crisis. *The Gardner Gazette* bellowed, "GARDNER LAKE SITE A SCENE OF GREAT ACTIVITY" followed by a long article listing the accomplishments. The project then employed 238 men "working cheerfully, particularly since the WPA took the project over," stated *The Gardner Gazette*. They went on to say that "the heat is terrific but so is the progress."

Late September brought heavy rains and Kill Creek was running "bank full." Men were positioned on the shore of the flume running under the dam and struggled with poles to keep the timber from choking the outlet. Until completion of the dam, estimated to be later that year, the basin could not be allowed to flood. In November, the earthwork for the dam was completed, and the remaining task was riprapping the sides with rock. Completion of the spillway was the daunting task at hand.

Diesel Power Shovel with Dragline
Preliminary work was in progress on the dam or spillway in late 1935. A worker looks on. (Photo courtesy of the Charles Rogers Collection, Gardner Historical Museum)

Howard's Agony

The treasurer for the Gardner Lake Corporation was Howard C. Bigelow, a cashier at Farmers Bank on Main Street. To him fell the task of acquiring the 350 acres of farmland needed for the construction of the lake. After several years of devastating crop failures and financial woes, this shouldn't have been a difficult task.

He acquired real estate contracts without too much difficulty for the nine tracts of land. Based on these signed commitments, the Kansas Forestry, Fish and Game Commission endorsed the project, and the Kansas Emergency Relief Committee moved forward with the camp construction and basin preparation. Things were in full swing while the corporation began selling lots to raise the funds to complete the land purchases.

After the 1934 real estate contracts were signed, but before closings were finalized, George W. Cristler, whose land was utilized to build the camp on what is now Lake Road 5, passed away. Cristler's widow was compliant, but her husband's share of the property passed by inheritance to three siblings; Lucy Black, P. V. "Tiny" Cristler and Mike Cristler. Evidently, Tiny signed without an issue, and Lucy agreed to transfer her deed upon Mike's agreement to do the same. Of the Cristler's 80-acre farm, the GLC agreed to buy 68 acres, leaving the family with 12.

What happened next was gut-wrenching. Evidently, seeing an opportunity to renegotiate his parent's arrangement, Mike Cristler upped the ante. Mike had moved to Boulder City, Nevada, to work on the construction of that dam, while Lucy now lived in Durant, Oklahoma, so correspondence moved at a snail's pace. At home, the KFFGC was breathing down Howard's neck for the deeds. Fourteen of the sixteen deeds were in hand, while the Cristler siblings were the two holdouts.

In a letter from Mike Cristler to Howard Bigelow dated May 7, 1934, Cristler demanded that the Gardner Lake Corporation dig a well or cistern on the remaining 12 acres. In Bigelow's reply of October 25, 1934, he agreed to that demand, in addition to providing three lake lots, free of charge. The GLC also agreed to provide cut firewood for a period of two years, if the Cristler's would return the deed signed, so that a closing could take place.

In a November 19, 1934 letter, Mike Cristler returned the deed unsigned and required Bigelow to reduce the size of an easement of 150 feet. The GLC agreed to reduce the easement to 25 feet, increasing the clearance between the Cristler barn and the common shoreline.

A letter from Bigelow dated March 20, 1936 assumed an almost pitiful tone. Having located Mike Cristler working at Coulee Dam in Washington, Bigelow wrote and explained how the KFFGC and the state continued to raise the requirements on the project. He went on to recount the water issues that required they build a water plant and a sanitation system. Bigelow referred to the KERC being disbanded and the WPA assuming control of the ongoing projects, leaving Gardner Lake caught in the lurch. He stated that the men were not very good workers, and that too much time was spent on the camp construction, resulting in the dam work being delayed. Basically, the project was over-budget and overdue. Bigelow advised Cristler that he had been forced to survey the land three times because of Cristler's demands. He reminded Cristler how he was now paying more for the property, while also providing $300 worth of lake lots. Then Bigelow stated, "Mike, the government notified us this morning that they were not going to do any further work on the dam until we delivered deeds to the property…". He noted that the lot owners are disgusted because the work is progressing so slowly.

Mike Cristler then issued a rather surly reply on March 29, 1936 saying that the GLC will need to buy the entire Cristler 80 acres, since his mother wanted to move to California, and the family did not need the land. He demanded $3,000 for the remaining acreage, an amount well-over market value. In a lengthy reply from Howard Bigelow on April 6, 1936, he stated, "The worry over this lake has taken about five years off my life and I would not go through it again for anything."

An August 12, 1936, letter from the Cristler's attorney announced that the contracts between the Cristler heirs and the GLC are being rescinded. A court summons was delivered to the GLC and project officials on September 10 with a suit brought for a permanent injunction and temporary restraining order for work being done on their property.

One can only guess what happened next, but the September 23, 1936 edition of *The Gardner Gazette* herald an article titled, "FULL SPEED AHEAD IN GARDNER LAKE PROJECT." The story declares that "…the misunderstanding has now, happily, been ironed out by the outright purchase of the Cristler eighty." The *Gazette* continued, "When the true story of the Gardner Lake is written, it will reveal a world of self-sacrifice, hard work, worry and the patient removal of obstacles from the pathway of the project."

Masonry Sub Wall of the Dam

The project required 1,920 square yards of masonry, such as this, with 9,500 square yards of 12" riprap, 4,500 square yards of 18" riprap (grouted) and 5,250 square yards of 18" riprap (clay). After 1,370 cubic yards of a crushed stone cushion, there are 750 cubic yards of loose riprap that are visible today above the water's edge. (Photo courtesy of the Olathe Public Library)

Dam Construction in 1937
This hand-built masonry wall was covered in loose riprap prior to water impoundment.
(Photo courtesy of the Charles Rogers Collection, Gardner Historical Museum)

Work Continues at the Gardner State Lake

At the opening of 1937, the WPA relocated an office from Olathe to the lake camp. Five people were employed there to manage the projects in Douglas and Johnson Counties.

The April 7 edition of *The Gardner Gazette* announced that the dam was complete, and that water was now being impounded. The spillway was still under construction, and given the years of drought, it was assumed that the filling process would be slow enough not to require the spillway for a considerable amount of time. An estimated twenty-five acres of water already collected behind the dam by that time.

According to folklore, there was a heavy rain during this period of the construction of the lake that flooded some heavy equipment parked in the lake basin near the dam. The crew decided to just leave it there under the water. This story has not been confirmed nor denied by evidence.

Spillway Construction
The unique spillway at Gardner Lake proved to be the biggest and most challenging aspect of the lake project. (Photo courtesy of the Charles Rogers Collection, Gardner Historical Museum)

Aerial View of Construction Site
This interesting aerial view of the lake, looking northwest, was taken after the completion of the dam and prior to the spillway in late 1936 or early 1937. Water has started to impound. Transient Camp 9 is visible in the lower left-hand corner. The Kill Creek bridge is still visible in the center of is photo. (Photo courtesy of the Gardner Historical Museum)

The Last Crossing of 159th Street

Richard McCreary, son of James and Florence Bray McCreary, was reared on his parent's dairy farm on 159th Street, west of the lake. The street was a busy dirt farm road that provided the best east and west crossing of the lake basin. The intersection of 159th and Gardner Road, before the latter was rerouted on the west side of the lake, was a low point that crossed Kill Creek.

McCreary recalls, as a lad of 4 or 5 years old, returning to their farm with his father traveling east to west on 159th near the Harrington property. Richard was riding in a hay rack behind the family's John Deere, knowing that there wasn't much that could get in their way.

By this time, the lake had started filling and they noticed that the low areas were already forming ponds with interlocking channels. It is then they saw the stream crossing the intersection at the lowest point. Not wanting to double back at sunset, they pressed forward. The water started to rise on the tractor, but it was not a problem, yet. As they pressed forward, the water got deeper and deeper. The wooden hay rack sat atop the chassis by virtue of gravity, and was otherwise not attached. As the water got deeper, the hay rack began to float off. Now submerged in four feet of water, James started to panic for fear of losing the hay rack and his son. The tractor suddenly lurched forward until it finally started to climb. Dripping safely on the steep west side of Gardner Road, they looked back and acknowledged that they were certainly the last two people who would make that crossing.

Looking Back

Kansas City Power and Light brought electricity to the east side of the lake and twinkling lights were visible at night.

April 18 was the big day for the prospective lot owners. The much-anticipated drawing for lot assignment took place at the camp mess hall with 2000 in attendance. The names of the people who purchased tickets were placed in a glass bowl. Miss Joan Stockmyer, the young granddaughter of R. J. "Bob" and Minnie Stockmyer, drew the names, which were then read aloud. The first name drawn was F. A. Kaserman of Overland Park. He purchased two lots and ended up with property on 152nd Street and a second lot on Lake Road 4. It is unknown which location was his first pick. Lot owners scrambled from the gathering to get a look at their new acquisition and cottages sprang up almost immediately.

Simultaneous to the selection of lots by ticket holders in April of 1937, the City of Gardner assumed the sponsorship of the project with the consent of the Kansas Forestry Fish and Game Commission. The Gardner Lake Corporation quit-claimed the property to the city.

The contributing buildings and elements started to appear. There would eventually be a beach house, a boat house, picnic shelters, the gazebo, referred to in the paper as a 'band stand,' a wellhouse, and latrines. There were twenty-three picnic "ovens" and twenty-six picnic tables dotted around the shoreline. Two additional rock wall dams were built to facilitate wading pools, one at the beach house and one below the dam in the big park. The park below the dam had a baseball diamond. There were plans for an ornamental stone bridge to cross the spillway, but that never materialized.

Latrine on Lake Road 10
The Gardner Lake Resort had a total of 12 latrines. They were built in pairs with one for women and one for men. A stone urinal was the only distinguishing difference. A handful of these survived in various stages of demolition or decomposition. One of these is still utilized as a foundation under the driveway at 16150 Gardner East Road. (Photo courtesy of Johnson County Archives)

Wading Pools Below the Dam
A series of wading pools enhanced the picnic area below the dam. (Photo by Buford Morrison, courtesy of the Gardner Lake Association)

Wellhouse Below the Dam
Park planners went to great lengths to have this building, located in the park below the dam, constructed with historic methods in 1937. The overhead beams were hand-hewed from massive logs joined together in the same method utilized during the construction of log buildings. It is the only building like that at the project. Two workers are barely visible inside. At some point, the well was capped with a layer of concrete. (Photo courtesy of the Charles Rogers Collection, Gardner Historical Museum)

LOOKING BACK

The May 12, 1937, edition of *The Gardner Gazette* reported that on the previous Sunday, crowds of people gathered at the lake. Much attention was drawn to the Kill Creek bridge that was located southeast of the dam on Gardner Road. The water was within two feet of the bridge deck.

The Kill Creek bridge was a landmark for years on Gardner Road. As the name implies, the road itself provided direct access to the town. It was graveled and only six feet wide at that time.

The Gardner Gazette indicated that the bridge, prior to becoming submerged, would be dismantled by the county and moved to another location. According to Glenn Bonar, life-long resident of the area, a fight broke out over the acquisition of the bridge between two local townships dealing with the deep ravines and creeks in their unincorporated areas. McCamish Township, just north of the lake, prevailed. It was reassembled in McCamish on 143rd Street between Kill Creek Road and Four Corners. Bonar said that some years after it was placed in position crossing Kill Creek once again, a Kansas City Power and Light Truck, with a trailer of huge wire spools, snagged the bridge so hard while traversing that it sent the truck, trailer, and bridge off its footings and into the creek. The road was closed for quite some time while the wreckage lay at the bottom of the ravine. It has been replaced by a modern concrete bridge. Currently, Bonar has elements of the original bridge on his farm. However, some remnants of the bridge may still be submerged. An article published in the June 6, 1952, edition of the *Kansas City Times* regarding the recovery attempt of a drowned victim, references the bridge at the bottom of the lake still. They stated that the remnants of the bridge, in addition to coils of cable, made the search effort extremely hazardous. Kenny Moll is adamant about seeing the bridge reappear during the extreme low-water conditions of 1954. So, the controversy continues.

> "A huge red bridge was transportation across the large expanse of water. I can still hear the creaking when vehicles drove over it."
>
> – Sadie McIntire-Powell,
> Gardner *Heritage*

WORK CONTINUES AT THE GARDNER STATE LAKE

Bunnee Rankin on Kill Creek Bridge

Frances L. "Shorty" Eastland props up T. Harold "Bunnee" Rankin on a trestle of the Kill Creek bridge on Gardner Road. This section of Gardner Road is now submerged under the mouth of Pirate's Cove. The road was rerouted along the west shore of the lake as part of the original project. This charming photo was probably taken in late 1936. (Photo courtesy of the Brad and Nancy Rankin family archives)

LOOKING BACK

Gardner Road was diverted west to circumnavigate the lake, and the original roadbed, running straight north and south, was then submerged.

On September 1, 1937, the paper reported that Jack Chesbro was transferred to the Lake Wabaunsee project near Eskridge. He was replaced by Shelby Jones as the project neared the 60 percent completion point.

Jack Chesbro Overseeing Progress Below Dam
This rare photo portrays Jack Chesbro observing the building of a stone bridge below the dam. There are scant remains of those stone steps surviving on the embankment at the west end of the park, with the remnants of two latrines as well. The stone bridge was engulfed by the water plant built there by the Department of Defense for the Olathe Naval Air Station in 1942. (Photo courtesy of the Linda Wedman Chesbro family archives)

The Stone Bridge
This stone bridge gave picnickers access to the park below the dam. (Photo courtesy of the Linda Wedman Chesbro family archives).

Work Continues at the Gardner State Lake

With plans for the dismantling of Transient Camp 9, officials decided that the fairgrounds in north Gardner could utilize the barracks buildings. With the additional capability those structures could provide, Johnson County considered relocation of the county fair from Olathe to Gardner. The lake and park would be an additional attraction for fair attendees.

Viewing the Beach from the Band Stand
This photo illustrates the bathing beach from the band stand on Lookout Drive (Lake Road 8). It was probably taken in the winter of 1938, and the piers for the boat house are visible just above the railing on the left edge of the photo. (Photo courtesy of the Gardner Lake Association)

LOOKING BACK

In early November of 1937, the beach house neared completion. Elaborate preparations were made to the grounds near the shoreline in anticipation of the arrival of tons of sand required to create the swimming area. Elsewhere on the lake, E. F. Alexander and Harry Eyerly took extreme measures to save indigenous oak trees that were dying as a result of persistent drought conditions. They drove holes in the rock-hard earth and insert small sticks of dynamite. The explosions that followed loosened the soil enough to accept the water they hand-carried to the site.

The shoreline around the lake was prepared for the foot path that would eventually encircle the lake. The ten-foot-wide path was accessible to the public by alleyways designated between certain plotted lots visible on the original maps. Below Lake Road 10, referred to as Block 6 and 7 at the time, evidence of these paths is still visible in places, although a capping of the spillway by the Navy in April of 1943 would raise the water level and submerge most of them.

Cottages on Outlook Drive
Two original cottages on Lake Road 9, known as "Outlook Drive" at the time, are still there today. This photo was taken from the north shore of Lake Road 5, below the tourists' cabins of the Gardner Lake Resort. The lake was still filling at the time of this photo. (Photo courtesy of the Gardner Lake Association)

Sailboat Moored in Pirates Cove

This photo shows the eastern most point of Pirate's Cove between Lake Road 11 and 12 in 1939. The gravel walking path that once encircled the lake is clearly visible in this photo. The cabin in this photo was demolished in 2020 and a modern home is now constructed there. (Photo by Buford Morrison, courtesy of the Gardner Lake Association)

Haderway Point

In this foreshortened photo, taken while the lake was filling, the bathing beach was under constriction (center right) and the remains of Gardner Road is visible in the distance. (Photo by Buford Morrison courtesy of the Gardner Lake Association)

LOOKING BACK

A comfortable residence was built at the lake for Shelby Jones, the camp superintendent who replaced Jack Chesbro. When the project was complete, the intention was that it would be occupied by the caretaker of the park. The one-story frame house had two small bedrooms and a galley kitchen. The central living room had a stone fireplace. It served as a residence for future lake managers and patrolmen. A second improvement to Gardner Road in the late 1960's would straighten out a dangerous curve in the street but claimed the original caretaker's house, which was then demolished.

The Caretaker's House

Many references to the Caretaker's House are made in KERA and WPA documents. It was provided for the Gardner Lake construction superintendent and eventually for the manager, then for the patrolmen, who would oversee the Gardner Lake Resort, as it came to be known. The location of the house was adjacent to the camp's north entrance on Lake Road 5, and at the time, the west side of Gardner Road on the west side of the lake. This would place it very near the beach house and the boat rental concession.

A 1939 receipt has survived, thanks to Gardner historian Claude Steed, who rescued discarded bank documents from the basement of the former Farmers Bank. The construction receipt states that the building was electrified with seven lights. In addition, the contractor, Mike Shannon, added a stone flue, repaired the front porch and screen, papered the roof, sanded and grooved barn boards for lining, sanded 500 square feet of granary boards for the flooring in the west room, and painted the north wall. The invoice total was $33.76 and was approved by E. F. Alexander.

A Gardner Road improvement project in the late 1960's straightened a curve in the road at the intersection of Lake Roads 4 and 5 that required the house be demolished.

Work Continues at the Gardner State Lake

1938 was ushered in with another major social event at the camp mess. Twelve-hundred birthday parties for FDR were planned nationwide for February 2. The event was a fundraiser for the treatment and cure of infantile paralysis, also known as polio, the dreaded disease that struck FDR down as a young man. A live orchestra from Lawrence provided a ball-like atmosphere for the evening gala.

Progress on the lake focused on the spillway in the spring of 1938. But elsewhere, the beach house was under construction with the beach ready for sand. The parameter roads were finished with a layer of gravel. Picnic grounds where then provided at every lake road that completed a circle.

As the lake neared completion, another major outdoor event was planned for the young park. Slated for May 22, 1938, officials announced plans for a celebration of the Gardner Lake Park project, the completion of the dam, and the near completion of the spillway. Although the lake was not ready for swimming or fishing, which was still prohibited at that time, the crowds were to be treated to an air show. However, extremely heavy rains caused the event coordinators to postpone the spectacle for two weeks.

Besides delaying the air show, the rains had a dramatic effect on the water level of the lake, which rose by an estimated twelve and a half feet. With sixteen feet still to go, the water was far below the base of the spillway. But lot owners could envision the final shape of the shoreline to great delight. The beach was partially covered, and many local boys were enjoying the first swimming, although it was unauthorized.

LOOKING BACK

The delayed event occurred on June 5, and an estimated crowd of 10,000 attended. Those in attendance were treated to impressive air maneuvers featuring low and fast flyovers and simulated air-to-air combat by the Army Reserve unit dispatched from Fairfax. Nearly over-flowing with people, the park below the dam accommodated a large Ferris wheel that stayed quite busy all day. A spirited baseball game between Adams Transfer and Gardner took place at the ball diamond near the arcade ride. The multiple picnic areas on the east side of the lake were carpeted with spectators while the Boy Scouts sold refreshments. A souvenir ashtray was struck showing the partially completed bathhouse, as the beach house was then referred, to commemorate the big event.

Souvenir Ashtray
This memento was given at the June 5, 1938, commemoration of the Gardner Lake Resort. Objects like this were probably made by the men at the camp in their down time. (Gift to the author by David Jackson. Photo courtesy of Sandy Adams, Adams ProPhoto)

July 4, 1938 brought another huge celebration at the lake. Although the daytime heat hovered around 103 degrees, and harvesting chores kept many farmers away, the event was an overall success. The night attendance made up the difference as folks were treated to a huge fireworks display. It was estimated that 4,000 people enjoyed the day and night festivities.

In September the spillway was completed, and the remainder of the efforts were spent finishing the beach house. Upon completion of the beach house, late in the year, the skilled stone masons turned their attention to a stone shelter house below the dam. That shelter house is still enjoyed today.

In early February 1939, Shelby Jones, camp superintendent, transferred to the WPA project at Fort Riley, and Don Griffing, construction engineer on the dam and spillway, retired. Things at Transient Camp 9 started to wind down as the major construction efforts were completed. All in all, the project cost the Federal government and local developers $567,245 in 2020 money, that represents an expenditure well over eleven million dollars, making it the largest of twelve WPA projects commissioned in Johnson County.

Willis Garnett Shanholtz

Undoubtedly, Gardner Lake's Transient Camp 9 was made up of colorful characters with unique stories. But one of the stonemasons, whose contributions are still evident today, may be the most fascinating.

W. G. Shanholtz was born in 1885, placing him in his early 50's when living at the state lake camp. One account of Shanholtz says he was from Hamilton, Canada, but in an interview he granted *The Kansas City Star* on June 17, 1962, he stated that he was born near Osceola, Missouri, in a cabin. However, his adventures as an adult made him a man of the world.

This story began to unfold towards the end of the lake project when he wrote to England for a copy of his discharge papers from the British Army. Evidently, this American won the Queen's *Medal of Valor* from Great Britain for his service during the South African Boer Wars at the opening years of the 20th century. As one of *Driscoll's Scouts*, a reconnaissance outfit, he heroically saved his squadron commander's life. His story was learned after he was interviewed by a young war correspondent named Winston Churchill. Shanholtz' distinction was unknown to him, however, until his discharge papers arrived 35 years later with the medal attached. (One account stated he was the only such recipient ever for the prize, which is only one degree below the coveted *Victoria Cross*). After the war, he was transferred to London, where he became part of the Queen's own *Royal Dragoons* and served for several years.

Proudly wearing a British medal, awarded for heroism in the Boer War, is W. G. Shanholtz, WPA stonemason of Gardner, Kan. The medal was officially awarded in 1904, but the British war office was unable to locate Shanholtz until he wrote for his discharge papers this year.

How would he have ended up there? Previously, Shanholtz was a groomer for equestrian Lula Long Combs. When she sold a number of horses to the British government, Shanholtz decided to accompany the horses on the freighter destined for South Africa in February 1899. Upon arrival, he disembarked at Port Elizabeth with this cargo and immediately enlisted in the *Royal Canadian Army*. Given the option of a six-month stint, or an enlistment for the duration of the war, he chose the latter and remained there for three years.

Assigned to the Imperial Light Horse Cavalry, Squadron E, Troop No. 2, Shanholtz saw some of the heaviest action of the war in three major engagements, including "Tigers Clouse," where the British were outnumbered eleven hundred to the Boer's six thousand. In the *Star* interview, Shanholtz stated, "We had to swim our horses across the river before we could attack, and the Boers were sniping at us from both sides and in the front. Many of our men sank in the river and never reached the bank. The battle lasted from 10 o'clock in the morning until about 8 at night. My horse was shot from under me. Only 108 of us escaped."

But that was just the beginning. With the conclusion of the Boer Wars in 1902, he found his way back to the States aboard the American liner *St. Louis*. Once home, Shanholtz immediately enlisted in the U.S. Marines and proceeded to Panama to aid in the construction of the canal. At one point, he even traveled west to become a cowpuncher.

His aunt once described Shanholtz as a world traveler and said that he would often vanish for years. How he ended up in Gardner is unknown, but when he left, in 1938, he moved to Denver to work for the Dowell Construction Company until 1950. With that firm, he traveled to Alaska to work on the highway between the Yukon border and Watson Lake.

There's a surviving photo that suggests he was married, but no other evidence. He retired to Osceola where he became a beloved fixture in town. He dressed in Western attire and had a collection of canes from all over the world that he alternately carried, although they weren't needed. He wore bolo ties with stones and a turquoise ring. He had a continental air about him and was nicknamed 'Churchill' by his admirers.

He died peacefully in Osceola in 1969, where he had taken up residency in a local hotel. Among his spartan possessions was a tintype of his mother who, sadly, had orphaned him early in life.

Work Continues at the Gardner State Lake

During the April rains, the lake rose two and one half feet. However, it would be a year later before the lake was finally considered full, and the spillway was utilized for the first time.

In the summer months of 1939, three of the barracks, affectionately known as 'huts', were removed and sold to the fairgrounds in Gardner for $250 each. Their contribution to the fairgrounds won Gardner the distinction of hosting the Johnson County Fair going forward. Although those buildings are now gone from the fairgrounds, the county fair continues to be a much-anticipated event every year in Gardner.

On January 1, 1940, *The Gardner Gazette* references "the abandonment of the Gardner Lake Camp". What remained at that time was the original, big rec and mess hall with kitchen, the water tower, and the thirteen tourist cottages.

The Johnson County Fairgrounds
In the late 1930s, several Transient Camp 9 buildings were rehomed to the fairgrounds to serve as exhibit halls. The availability of the buildings and the proximity of the lake helped Gardner win the distinction of having the permanent location for the popular annual event. The fair had previously been held in Olathe. (Photo courtesy of the Olathe Public Library)

Huts on the Move

Never intended as permanent structures, the wooden barracks buildings of Transient Camp 9 still offered substantial utility long after their inhabitants had scattered in 1939. The first stop on their cross-town trip was the Johnson County fairgrounds just north of downtown Gardner at Elm and Shawnee Streets. They were utilized as exhibit displays for no less than 40 years as they continued to appear prominently in photos taken in the 1970's. From there they were sold or given to citizens for sheds and farm buildings. The remains of two of those structures are still barely evident on the west side of Center Street, near 186th Street, where they have now collapsed and have been engulfed by trees and brush. However, Dave Bryan, who resides at the southern-most spot on the lake, has carefully maintained his hut as an outbuilding on the family property. He dismantled half of the structure to provide materials to repair the remaining half. The condition of the remaining half betrays its age. If only buildings could talk.

The camp "huts" were not the only buildings that were moved to and from here. There are several duplexes sold from the older housing complex at Sunflower Army Ammunition Plant, known as Sunflower Village. These duplexes were sold off in 1955 after ads appearing in the July editions of *The Gardner News* boasted of a liquidation sale at the Sunflower Village Housing Project. These 21'X 52' duplexes were available for $895, and 21' X 42' duplexes were only $795. The ad stated "These houses have asbestos sheet siding, good roofs, oak floors and sheetrock." One is located at 16050 Lake Road 6 (Gardner East Road). The home at 15655 Lake Road 4, occupied by Darlene Prier until her recent passing in 2021, is another example.

The Gardner Gazette reported in their August 13, 1941, edition that Paul A. Speckin purchased the tenant house from the Gallanaugh farm to move to the lake. The family enjoyed that house until it was razed by fire in 1955. A year later, they purchased a Sunflower duplex and moved it to its current location at 15349 Lake Road 2. After the addition of a porch and other upgrades, it isn't recognizable as a former solution to a housing crisis.

According to Mrs. John T. Patty, a columnist for *The Gardner Gazette* and later *The Gardner News* in the early 1940's, the old Splinterville one-room schoolhouse was moved to Lake Road 1, where it was repurposed as a lake cottage. The Splinterville School was formerly located a few miles west of Edgerton. Elsewhere on the lake, the *Gardner News* reported in its August 24, 1944, edition that "Mr. Wm. Gould was moving a small house to his lot," and that a small house from Fairfax was being moved by F.J. Eils, presumably, to his lot at 29290 W. 155th Terrace, now vacant. The Eils remained at the lake until sometime after 1966.

PART II

The Gardner Lake Resort Years
1938-1970

Chapter 7

ORDINANCE 518 - LAYING DOWN THE LAW

On May 7, 1940, the Gardner City Council met to establish the "dos and don'ts" for "Gardner Lake Park," as it was referred to then. The ordinance regulated both the park area as well as recreation on the lake. It provided for the issuing of licenses and permit fees, as well as establishing the penalty for violating the regulations.

In addition to the state ordained licensing, the city required a license for fishing. For example, Johnson County residents paid fifty cents a day per person, or five dollars for the season. Non-county residents paid one dollar a day or seven dollars and fifty cents for the season. The fees were waived for lake lot owners, who were still required to be licensed by the state. Lot owners could procure guest permits to the tune of two dollars and fifty cents for the season. Children under the age of fifteen could fish for free as long as they were accompanied by an adult. Folks over the age of seventy were exempt as well, and needless to say, didn't need adult supervision. Permit holders were limited to one rod and line with not more than two hooks, or a fly rod and line with not more than two flies. Casting rods were not allowed to have more than one artificial bait or lure attached. Also, there would be no trot lines, set lines, flat, bank or limb lines. Daily catch limits were established as

Ordinance 518 - Laying Down the Law

well. No person could take more than ten game fish a day with bass limited to five, and a minimum length of ten inches. Up to five channel cat could be kept as long as they were at least twelve inches long. To be keepers, crappie were required to be at least seven inches long. Blue gill and perch needed to be six inches in length. An angler may take from the lake a maximum of twenty bullheads a day. One was required to wet your hands before handling the fish to be released.

Seining, trapping or netting minnows for bait was also not permitted. And dumping live bait into the lake was a violation as well. Only daylight fishing was permitted.

No hunting or trapping of any kind was permitted. In fact, no firearms were allowed whatsoever on the park property.

Boats required a permit as well. Outside of the lake patrol boat, no gasoline powered boats were permitted. However, electric boats were allowed as long as they operated on battery only. Sailboats and canoes required a license as well. County residents paid fifty cents a day or five dollars per season. Non-residents paid one dollar a day or seven dollars and fifty cents, respectively.

Herb Klemp and his Electric Boat

This charming photo, taken on July 4, 1945, shows Herb Klemp with family and friends at the helm of his electric boat with his favorite pet Mitzi. Gasoline powered motors were not permitted until May 1950. In the background is Lake Road 4. (Photo courtesy of the Herb and Helen Klemp family archives)

The ordinance allowed for a boat rental concession to be managed by the custodian or employees hired for that purpose. Row boats were rented for fifty cents for a minimum of two hours or one dollar a day. Occupancy was limited to two people per boat.

Swimming permits were sold for ten cents a day or two dollars for the season. Children under the age of ten, who were accompanied by an adult, were free as were lake lot owners. But exemptions for lot owners was limited to one per household.

Lot Owner's Swimming Privilege Card
This wallet-size card was recovered at 15516 Lake Road 10 during a renovation. (Courtesy of Cindy Derosa)

Ordinance 518 made provisions for the city to hire up to three custodians to collect fees and cut permits. This person, or persons, also managed the boat rental concession at all the Gardner Lake Park properties. Finally, the ordinance established the fines for violating its provisions. The perpetrator would be guilty of a misdemeanor and punished by a fine of no less than five dollars and no more than one hundred dollars. Or they might be incarcerated in the city prison or county jail for a period not to exceed thirty days. A heinous act could justify both a fine and jail time. The bottom of the document contains the signature of the major, Charles Cramer and R. K. Stockmyer, city clerk.

During this period, the first of many lake property owner advocacy groups emerged. The Gardner Lake Lot Owners Association is first mentioned in a city document on May 11, 1941, when they met with city officials at the Gardner Lake Resort clubhouse. Mayor Higgins with Councilmen J. S. Cordell, C. S. McCreary and Dr. A. S. Reece negotiated with the group

Ordinance 518 - Laying Down the Law

to allow paid-up association members to have transferable guest fishing permits at a cost of two dollars per season, not to exceed five permits for each member. They also agreed that paid-up association members were not required to ante an additional fee for any lake privileges. In exchange, the association would pay one hundred dollars annually into the Gardner Lake Fund, a budget line item, of which fifty dollars would be allocated to weed control and fifty dollars towards maintenance of the "swimming pool" at the bathing beach. This was made law in the form of Ordinance 519.

Ordinance 536, introduced and signed into law on March 1, 1948, contained the usual permit fee structures and set fishing limits, but it took things a bit farther. Section 9 reads verbatim, "SWIMMING. It shall be unlawful for any person to swim in said Lake." That simply prohibited swimming altogether.

On May 7, 1950, Ordinance 546 finally made allowances for gasoline powered boat motors as long as they were limited to three horsepower. Although it repealed Ordinance 536, it contains no reference to swimming.

Finally, on December 7, 1957, ordinance 713 references swimming with a permit, but doesn't reference the costs or parameters of such. The three-horsepower restriction on gasoline motors is removed with the stipulation that there is no racing. Boating operations were limited to fishing only between one half hour before sunrise to one half hour after sunset. Evidently, the ordinance didn't go far enough defining boat operations and wasn't well enforced. Lake activity often included water skiing, according to the local newspaper.

Members of the Gardner Lake Improvement Association, the current advocate group for the residents at the time, compelled the mayor to sign Ordinance 725 on June 20, 1958, which limited speed limits to five miles per hour. It fell short of the group's demand to permit the use of boats "for the convenience of lake residents" and the request for the boat's occupant capacity be painted on its hull.

Finally, on May 24, 1965, ordinance 888 established the ten-mile-per-hour speed limit that exists today.

Chapter 8
OPENING DAY FOR FISHING FINALLY ARRIVES

If you were an angler back then, the day you had been anxiously awaiting was May 15, 1940. That cold and dreary Wednesday morning marked the very first day for fishing at Gardner State Lake. Any fishing prior to that date was considered poaching, and a patrolman enforced that restriction. But on that memorable morning, officials felt the fish were finally mature enough to become the object of sport.

A temporary headquarters opened at the northwest end of the dam staffed with three people to handle the enormous demand for fishing licenses. A starting signal fired early that morning, which unleashed a frenzy of casting and reeling. Incidentally, *The Gardner Gazette,* in their May 15, 1940, edition, made special mention of the fact that the first fish snatched from the lake was caught by a woman. Her name was Mrs. U. F. Ewing, (in other words, you still don't know her name, you just know her husband's name).

Coincidentally, perhaps, on the 26th of the following month, the city council convened to pass Ordinance 519, which revisited the cost of fishing licenses. From that day going forward, the fee for women would be half the price of those for men. Presumably, women were not considered capable as anglers, or more likely, they couldn't possibly have time for a relaxing sport therefore couldn't be a burden on the population of the lake's stock.

The Story of Fishburger

In the 1940's, a father and son team, James Manning Sr. and James Manning Jr., were known around Gardner by their obsession with fishing at the Gardner Lake Resort. Jim Sr. was a popular citizen of Gardner, and Jim Jr., a court stenographer in Olathe, had a house on Lake Road 9 at what is now 29325 W. 155th Terrace. Jim Sr. was no stranger to the lake. He built one of the original cottages, and through the years, built several more. The son's proximity to the lake, a few doors east of the gazebo, provided lots of opportunities for them to share their passion for the sport. The paper reported that Jim Jr., or Jimmy as he was referred, would trade catfish for chicken, pound for pound, with friends in town. Together, they concocted their own bait formula in junior's kitchen.

In the January 24, 1946, edition of *The Gardner News*, the guys created what was literally, a 'cottage industry.' The paper reports that "Out at Lake Gardner-almost under our nose, but not quite fortunately, has sprung up a flourishing business in the last year." They stated the team converted the cottage to a factory with rows of electric mixers lined up to manufacture "Fishburger," a bait for catfish.

After they marketed the bait in the *Kansas City Star*, hundreds of orders came flooding into the post office. An 82-year-old man in Balke, Oklahoma reordered three times. In one of his orders, he said "Send two more boxes of the bait." He said he "…had to put (it) on the hook while I hid behind a tree to keep the fish from stealing it out of the box."

In June of 1946, the paper reported the angler entrepreneurs were even publishing a "well edited magazine known as the *Fishburger News*." It was distributed to sporting dealers all over the states who were handling their product. It was full of information, including fishing tips and recipes. There were even some fish stories, as one would imagine. Jimmy had attended classes in journalism and the results of his efforts was evidently well-written. His articles were reprinted in many sports magazines, according to *The Gardner News*.

They were very successful, actually. The Manning family operated it for eight years until they received an offer too good to refuse. L. A. Miller, Sr., and L. A. Miller, Jr. of Kansas City purchased the business in 1953. It lived on as another family affair.

On September 3, 1953, a FOR SALE ad appeared in the local paper for Jimmy's house at Gardner Lake. It read, "2 bedroom year-round modern home on Gardner Lake, $6500.00 -James G. Manning, Jr., Lake Road 9, phone 177R."

Coincidentally in 1953, the Kansas State Fish and Game Commission felt compelled to consign 1400 channel cat, between 8" to 10" in length, to Gardner Lake from Kanapolis Lake, in the hopes of replenishing the stock. These young fish matured in the following year. Maybe there really was something to the 'Fishburger Bait.'

LOOKING BACK

Through those early years, fishing was the lake's main attraction. The presence today of extravagant fishing boats on the water would indicate that little may have changed. Articles describing extraordinary successes by anglers were not uncommon in the local paper, like this one which appeared on July 27, 1961, when lake resident Paul Grahovac grabbed his shiny new rod and reel and headed to the water for some sport. He hooked a formidable specimen three times, and three times his line broke. In frustration, he grabbed is old cane pole and some heavier line, a tiny hook and a big worm. Within minutes, the fish was back on the line and Paul was in for a half hour of fun. When he finally wrestled the beast to the surface, he saw a huge, whiskered mouth glittering with hooks. It was a 20-pound catfish that measured thirty-seven and one quarter inches in length. All of Grahovac's lost tackle was returned, and he earned the nickname 'Harold Ensley of Gardner Lake' by his fellow workers at the Delco battery plant in Olathe.

Walter Stempski's Stringer
This photo was taken behind the family cottage on Gardner East Road. (Photo courtesy of the Delores Gribbin family archives)

Opening Day for Fishing Finally Arrives

Folklore has it that there are six-foot-long catfish in the depths of the lake. This is fiction according to Ed Hayes, retired law enforcement officer for the Johnson County Sheriff's Department and a member of their dive team. He says that the divers from the Naval Air Station stated that after searching for a drowned victim. Hayes, who is well-familiar with the bottom of the lake, says that the largest catfish he ever saw was around four feet in length. He found it on one of his diving adventures living in the remains of a fifty-five-gallon barrel of which the ends had been knocked off. It was longer than the container and was sticking out on both ends. His curiosity got the best of him, and he decided to bring it ashore to weigh it. Hayes capped one end and threw a net over the other. He was shocked at what happened next. To his surprise, that fish blew out the side like a rocket being launched. That was the last he saw of it.

Herb Klemp, who has also explored the bottom of the lake, said that the bottom is covered in a thick layer of fish line and that no one should dive it alone, and certainly shouldn't dive it without a sharp knife.

Herb's Fine Catch
Heinie, Herbie and Mimi Klemp proudly show off Herb's catfish behind their stone cottage on Lake Road 8 in this 1950 photo. (Courtesy of the Herb and Helen Klemp family archives)

Chapter 9
THE PUBLIC BEACH

In June 1937, the Gardner Lake Corporation quitclaimed all the lake property to the City of Gardner with the state retaining the water rights. With this transition, the city operated the lake assets for profit or pleasure, at their discretion.

In 1938, when the lion's share of the project was complete, the public beach opened on Lake Road 4 for its first season. The bathhouse was one of the last structures of the mammoth lake project to be completed and preceded only the shelter house in the park below the dam. Irene Peer, who attended one of the first big camp celebrations in 1935, said that the beach house and gazebo were built by two Irish brothers who were expert stone masons. The fact that the stone masons were experts is obvious.

The Bader Family at the Beach
Although the Bader family owned a cottage on Lake Road 10, they still enjoyed outings at the beach. (Photo courtesy of the Bader family archives)

The Public Beach

Original plans showed the bathhouse and beach on Lake Road 5 adjacent to the camp. However, it was assumed that the water depth couldn't accommodate the construction of the boathouse, so during planning, the popular spot was relocated to its current location on Lake Road 3. Little is known of the boathouse. The house at 15485 Lake Road 4, the first house south of the beach, was built on that location, and possibly encompasses that structure.

The Bathhouse from an Interesting Vantage Point
This Buford Morrison photo was taken looking southwest.
(Photo courtesy of the Gardner Lake Association)

When The Lake was Finally Full

It's hard to imagine that anyone could know exactly when the lake was finally full. But evidently, *The Gardner News* felt they had it nailed as May 18, 1940.

Here's what they had to say in their May 22nd edition:

> "Between five and six o'clock, Saturday evening of last week, a tiny rivulet of water threaded its way uncertainly along the floor of the spillway of the Gardner Lake, paused momentarily here and there, as its course was impeded by stones and earth, and, as its level increased, pushed forward until, with increasing speed, it finally joined the waters of the creek below the dam. But no vast volume of water poured down the spillway."

The city fathers seemed somewhat conflicted or indecisive regarding swimming at the lake. Ordinance 518 of June 1940 allowed for swimming at the bathing beach only, and only when there was a lifeguard on hand. That lifeguard may have been Mr. L. R. Schmutz, according to the June 5, 1940, edition of *The Gardner Gazette*.

In April of 1943, while World War II raged on, the Gardner City Council struck a deal with ONAS for the Navy to take over the swimming facilities at the lake. The Navy immediately banned swimming anywhere on the lake except at the beach, and that was limited to certain days at specific times. Those swimmers had to possess a card issued by the Navy and signed by the city clerk granting them permission. Then a fee of 10 cents for kids and 25 cents for adults was required. Lake lot owners were exempt from the fee. The Navy had full control of the lake with guards and sentries for enforcement. This peculiar arrangement was probably in response to threats of sabotage of the ONAS' water supply. It was during that period that Shore Patrol controlled traffic across the dam from both approaches.

The Public Beach

Ordinance 536, signed into law on March 1, 1948, prohibited swimming anywhere on the lake, one might assume, for fear of drownings. However, Glenn Bonar, life-long resident, recalls that the swimming ban was imposed due to a recent outbreak of polio. Evidently, there was no exception for lot owners. The vacated bathhouse created an attraction for the Navy boys, who turned it into their private party venue, Bonar said. Herb Klemp vaguely remembers the swimming ban and said that they ignored the ordinance and swam at will. Being a dock owner, he and his friends had no need to use the bathing beach anyway. On June 6, 1956, Ordinance 681 finally allowed swimming in designated areas, specifically the bathing beach. It continued to ban swimming anywhere else, but it must have been widely ignored by lot owners as few legacy residents remember the restriction.

Herb Klemp Ignores the Ban on Swimming
There was a ban placed on swimming at the lake in 1948, presumably due to the polio epidemic. With a private dock, there was little concern of being caught by officials. (Photo courtesy of the Herb and Helen Klemp family archives)

LOOKING BACK

During those years, the City of Gardner leased the beach operation out to a local operator. In 1959, Jim Westhoff leased the property during his summer break from KU for $500 for the season, which started on Memorial Day and ended on Labor Day. He opened the beach at 10:00 am and closed it at 8:30 pm. Westhoff was required to keep lifeguards on duty whenever there were swimmers. A large display ad in the local paper announced its opening in early June. Admission for children was twenty-five cents and thirty-five cents for adults.

Jimmie Shippee Enjoys the Beach
Evidently the ban was not taken seriously as this 1948 photo would suggest. The Shippee family has deep roots in Gardner and at Gardner Lake. (Photo courtesy of the Jim Shippee family archives)

Enjoying the Shallow Section
The Gardner Lake Resort beach was a favorite spot for kids as evident in this 1952 photo. Sparsely populated Lake Road 10 is in the background. (Photo courtesy of Faith Sterling family archives)

The Public Beach

Al Breitenstein enjoys a swim in this photo from the 1940's
Taken from the east shore, the Beach House swim dock is clearly in the background. (Photo courtesy of Francie Locke Family Archives)

Typical Summer Weekend at the Beach
(Photo courtesy of the Gardner Historical Museum)

Looking Back

When Westhoff's parents, Clyde and Susan, saw how lucrative it was, they leased it from the city in 1961 and continued to do so for a decade.

Many local adolescents were hired to serve as lifeguards, including Gary Winters, who worked there in 1957 and 1958. Pete Adams Sr. worked there in 1959. Adams recalls the lifeguard tower positioned midway between the wading beach and the deep water, which was identified by a rope with floats. Swimmers had to demonstrate their skill before the guards would let them cross those ropes, 150 feet from shore, and swim to the diving dock. It was reported that an abrupt drop from the shallow end to the deep part was between ten and twenty-five feet making those ropes essential for non-swimmers. Larry Keegan also served as a lifeguard during that time. Larry said that much of his time was spent chasing the little kids back to the shallow end.

Richard McCreary recalls an anchored fence surrounding the entire beach area. He says his cousin, Don Bray, bragged about finding a hole in the fence. The two of them swam from the east side across the lake and through the fence to skirt the ticket fee.

Gene and Roberta Gay ran the operation from 1972 to 1974. Two of their daughters served as lifeguards. Jody Gay remembers saving three lives there with two rescues within ten minutes of each other. During the holiday weekends, five lifeguards could be kept very busy; at least three at a time. Roberta remembers that a lot of Kansas City Kansans made the trip to the lake. She said it was very popular among motorcyclists who appeared threatening, but really weren't.

Mike and Dorothy Rattenne ran the operation for the last thirteen years. Although it was a lot of work, like the Gays and Westhoffs, it was a family labor of love. Their three children, Mitzi, Tammy and Mike Jr., all served as lifeguards and swim instructors. Dot recalls that, when they acquired the operation, there was a problem with a couple groups of "roughnecks" who came out from Olathe. They swam over from the east shore and skipped the gate, then vandalized the dock and diving boards. Mike, Jr., on summer

The Public Beach

break from K.U., brought four of his friends out to work with him. Together they cleaned the place up, both literally and figuratively, and threw the punks out for good.

Tammy befriended a goose named Alexander. She taught Alexander to give her a kiss when she put her cheek near his beak. A picture of the stunt ended up in several newspapers, nationally.

Dot fondly remembers a group of Croatians who traveled out from Strawberry Hill in Kansas City, Kansas to enjoy the beach in the summers. "They were super nice people," Dots recalls, and would bring the Rattenne's wonderful baked goods.

In 1989, the city of Gardner demanded that the Rattenne's plumb the bathhouse for hot water, presumably because they were preparing and selling food. They reluctantly gave up the operation, which marked its permanent closing. The City of Gardner contemplated the sale of the property with the stipulation that the purchaser demolish the building. That requirement created much controversy as residents could not envision the lake without their beloved bathhouse. Two energetic Gardner Lake Association members, Marg Leitner and Barbra Jacoby, mobilized and circulated a petition. They also went through the exhausting nomination process for historical recognition through the Kansas State Historical Preservation Office. The results compelled the state to list the property on their historic register, which then triggered its inclusion on the National Register of Historic Places on May 4, 1992. The distinction was granted due to the historical value of the "New Deal" era of relief, in addition to its recognition as a significant example of period architecture and construction.

The involvement of the Kansas State Historical Society was not welcomed by the city, who reluctantly removed the demolition requirement and opened the bidding process for the sale of the property. In May of 1992, Bill Bonds won the bid with an offer of $30,100 for the structure and the two and one-half acres adjacent. His intention was to convert the property to a restaurant or a clubhouse for the golf course, he told *The Gardner News* at the time. Evidently, neither transpired.

Looking Back

Today the bathhouse is in the loving care of private owners and is often the site of enthusiastic summer activities reminiscent of its robust history.

The Iconic Bathhouse
This Buford Morrison photo was taken at the end of 1938 or early 1939. Lake Road 10, known as Scout Drive, is in the background. In the far distance is a Transient Camp 9 barrack building, probably moved there to facilitate the workers completion of the fixtures at the park. The footpath is clearly visible. (Photo courtesy of the Gardner Lake Association)

A Magnificent Structure

The beach house was built in the 'rustic style' as mandated by the National Park Service. The local limestone was skillfully laid in an intricate random ashlar pattern. The interlocking appearance of the wall stone displays evidence of the presence of skilled stonemasons at the project. An unusual cartouche on the chimney of the massive fireplace is also visible in the stonework on the park shelter house. Those stones appear to have been found while constructing the canal behind the spillway wall itself. Their goal of achieving a harmonious union between building and landscape was completely achieved when painters finished the wood trim in warm brown tones.

Originally designed as two large changing rooms, with the boys' on the north of the structure and the girls' on the south, it also had a counter for ticket sales. Swimmers would pay their admission of .50 cents for adults and .25 cents for kids. Children under the age of five were free when accompanied by an adult.

A patio with a gabled roof was open on three sides facing the lake with a window to access concessions. From there, swimmers could purchase hamburgers, hotdogs, chips and candy. In the 1970's you could also rent innertubes and float boards.

The bathing beach soon became the central spot for family and social recreation for people of all ages. Tanning teens and adults could enjoy the diving dock with its double platform while children waded out on the shallow, sandy grade, but not into the deep water.

Chapter 10

BOAT RENTALS

In addition to swimming, the lake also offered boat rentals from a boathouse south of the beach. There, small rowboats were available to accommodate two passengers for the purpose of fishing. A portion of the original boat dock is still in use behind the present home at 15485 Lake Road 4. The rugged pipe framework of the dock shows the effect of the elements but has otherwise stood the test of time.

Rental Boat Number 113
The Gardner Lake Resort boat rental concession was located adjacent to the south of the beach. In 1942, these two passenger boats rented for $1.00 a day or $.50 for half a day. Hourly rental was $.25. (Photo courtesy of the Johnson County Archives)

BOAT RENTALS

Interestingly, Phil Keegan lived in this house in the late 1950's. His son, Larry, reports that a section of the original house used to be positioned much closer to the water but was moved back to its current footprint years ago. Therefore, the oldest section of this house on Lake Road 4 may have been part of the original boathouse concession.

In 1942, the boat operation was run by Tom Roesser, who could always advise you of the quality of the fishing that day. The boats were rented for a dollar a day, fifty cents for a half day or twenty-five cents an hour. Next to the boathouse was a large picnic area where people frequently cooked their fresh catch on the stone fireplaces, or ovens as they were referred at the time.

It is unknown how long the rental operation lasted. In the late 1940's, boats were still being offered for rent, although there may have been temporary interruptions when the manager's position was vacant for short periods. A large display ad as late as the April 26, 1956 edition of the local paper boasted that, under new management, there were boats available to rent and live bait to sell. But, at this point, no later reference to boat rentals has been found.

Chapter 11
GARDNER LAKE RESORT

The entire lake complex was known as 'Gardner Lake Resort' for a good reason. The scenic parameter of the lake was dotted with multiple, well-groomed picnic areas complete with the stone fixtures. The shoreline had walking trails with public access and a rustic, split-rail fence meandered along the boundary for six miles. Real estate classified ads in the *Kansas City Star* and the *Kansas City Times* proudly boasted that the location of the property was the 'Gardner Lake Resort.'

The March 3, 1947 edition of *The Gardner News*, said this about the Gardner Lake Resort:

> "Gardner has the only fishing lake in Johnson County, 160 acres of blue water to a depth of 60 feet, and five miles of shoreline studded with many native trees in a natural setting among which are occupied. We should be getting acquainted with all of these people, too. Below the dam at the lake is a shelter house for picnickers and a filtration plant where water is purified for use at the Olathe Naval Base. Picnic ovens and tables abound in numbers, and latrines, constructed of native stone, are numerous. The first warm days

GARDNER LAKE RESORT

of spring will call people to this picnic ground of the county, and they will continue to come until cold weather. Buildings owned by the city include ten cabins, a five-room residence, and a building approximately 60' X 100', now being operated by J. R. Bernhardt as a dance hall and refreshment stand; and a club house which is now occupied by the American Legion."

Jon Rueck Prepares the Catch of the Day
Twenty-three of these stone, cook ovens dotted the multiple parks that ran the perimeter of the lake. This photo was taken in 1954 at a picnic with Arnie Johnson and friends. (Photo courtesy of the Arnold Johnson family archives)

Chapter 12
GARDNER LAKE RESORT CLUBHOUSE

Eventually, with the closing of Transient Camp 9 in 1939, the city decided to repurpose the large central mess and rec hall on Lake Road 5. In mid-June of 1940, the first reference to the Gardner Lake Resort Clubhouse, as it was deemed, appeared in the local paper with the gathering there of the L.G.L. club on a Thursday night for a dance. The first manager was Wayne Newall.

Meeting of The Rural Life Club
The Gardner Lake Resort clubhouse was a popular venue for numerous clubs and organizations. This group met here in 1940. (Photo courtesy of the Johnson County Archives)

Gardner Lake Resort Clubhouse

The large mess hall was the perfect venue for parties and dances. But Newall added a roller rink to the venue, which opened on October 18, 1941, to the delight of area children. Two months later, *The Gardner Gazette* reported that he subleased the operation to a Mrs. Cook.

Roller Skating Rink

I am opening a roller skating rink at the Gardner Lake Resort and will be ready to serve you on Saturday, Oct. 18. First-class skates and perfect floor. Admission, 20c, plus tax.

W. R. NEWELL, MANAGER

The Gardner News, October 15, 1951
(Image courtesy of *The Gardner News*)

As a popular forum for club meetings and venue for parties, the American Legion made the camp building their home as well. *The Gardner Gazette* mentioned in their September 2, 1942, edition that, "Over three hundred sailor lads and their girlfriends were guests of Mr. and Mrs. Brown at the Lake Resort Club House Saturday at a dancing party."

In 1947, *The Gardner News* advertised that a dining room was now open at the resort. The menu offered fried chicken, baked sugar-cured ham and sandwiches. On Saturday evenings, they featured popular bands with dancing. Ralph Reese, son of Mr. and Mrs. Ebb Reese, cabin owners at the lake, entertained at the resort with his orchestra between 1947 and 1948. In 1952, their cabin at Lake Road 11 and 10, was reported to be the only one with plastered walls and wallpaper. However, the end of 1947 seemed to mark the end of another failed attempt for the venture.

Ordinance 560, published on March 8, 1951, authorized the mayor, Shelby Jones, to enter into a lease agreement "for the maintenance and operation of a café and dance hall as well as ten (10) cabins adjacent to said café building, known and referred to as Gardner Lake Resort, for a period of ten years." The ordinance sets the wages at fifty dollars in cash at the first of every month, plus fifteen dollars a month commission for every "new" cabin that was rented and tens dollars for the "old" cabins.

The Gardner News, November 27, 1947
The Gardner Lake Resort clubhouse managers suffered many failed endeavors through the years. (Image courtesy of *The Gardner News*)

The Gardner Lake Resort even sponsored a basketball team in the American Legion basketball tournament as the "Lake Resort" team, likely comprised of Navy seamen. During the 1951 season, they played and defeated such teams as The Marines, Gardner Boosters, Edgerton, DeSoto, Roark Motors, Olathe Merchants and Osawatomie. The Gardner Lake Resort was an important social point for the sailors from ONAS. The manager of the resort was Clifford C. Cravens, hired April 1, 1951. He was responsible for blowing the whistle when ONAS inadvertently leaked lubricants into the lake a year later.

Ordinance 631 replaced Cravens with Guy Ranney, a retired chief petty officer from Little Rock, on August 4, 1953. For the first time, the ordinance refers to eight rental cabins instead of ten. The last two ordinances were signed into law by Mayor Neil "Cot" Cordell, former transportation provider at Transient Camp 9.

To Ranney's credit, he worked hard to promote the resort. For the summer months of 1953, their display ads dominated the front page of the paper for the first time. The resort was a 'Teen Town Tavern' every Friday night (alcoholic beverages strictly prohibited, and a matron on duty). For Saturday night there was dancing to orchestra music for one dollar and fifty cents per couple (door prizes for ladies). They sponsored the "Sunrise Dance" on September 7, that started at midnight, with music from Bob Blum's Orchestra, and continued into the morning hours. They also hosted the "Hobo Party," which initiated underclassmen to Gardner High School, a few days later. The Ranney's offered the venue for free to the teens and gave door prizes for the best costumes.

Kenny Moll, whose family has farmed north of Gardner since 1902, recalls Ranney in fond terms and held him in high regard. Moll, graduate of Gardner High School class of '52, set up chairs and tables, with the help of his friends, for events in the large assembly room. In exchange, they were given free run of a back room for their teen functions. Ranney kept sleeping quarters in a room at the southwest corner of the building to save him a commute home to Olathe, Moll remembers.

In 1954, a terrible drought year, there is no mention of Gardner Lake Resort in *The Gardner News*. Not a single ad appeared in the paper. In fact, there was virtually nothing said about the lake at all. Very low water levels made the atmosphere unpleasant at the park areas. Fishing was certainly curtailed due to boat docks resting on mud, and the deep-water area at the bathing beach was probably a muddy quagmire.

But the conspicuous absence of the clubhouse promotion may have also been in part due to the possibility that Ranney's health was failing. He died on December 5, 1954, at Veteran's Hospital in Little Rock while on a visit. There was no mention of the cause of death, however. Aside from siblings, it appeared he had no family. There was no flowery obituary to honor the man who brought enjoyment to so many adults and adolescents at the Gardner Lake Resort.

At some point in 1955, the resort clubhouse lease was picked up by Bert Mathes, Jefferson City, who then handed the daily operation to his nephew or son, Marion 'Mike' L. Mathes, who lived at the lake, possibly at the resort.

Raid at Gardner Lake Resort

The Gardner Lake Resort was a favorite watering hole for the sailors and officers based at nearby Olathe Naval Air Station. And, with so many lake cottages in the hands of these military people, the convenience factor must have been very compelling. Therefore, it seemed like the obvious venue for the Olathe VFW when planning a stag party in 1955.

At the time, conservative Kansas had strict liquor laws that limited the sale of alcoholic beverages to that of 3.2 beer in licensed establishments such as the Gardner Lake Resort club house. And gambling was not permitted under any circumstances anywhere in the state. But Marion L. "Mike" Matthes, who operated the resort, evidently decided to turn a blind eye to the veterans the night of August 27. And why not? These were the heroes who saved the world only a decade ago. Mike himself, was an Army veteran.

The Gardner Lake Resort was a favorite spot for kids during the day when it doubled as a roller rink, teen town and community center. But apparently it transformed at night and was starting to get a rather dubious reputation as a rowdy honky-tonk. The resort had found itself on the radar of the state attorney general's office. Acting on a tip, Will Johns, veteran investigator for the state office, along with one of his colleagues, purchased two $1.00 tickets to attend the party at 9:30 that evening. The tickets indicated that the party was sponsored by the Olathe V.F.W. post No. 2993, and that there was a raffle and a floor show to be held at 9:45 that evening.

Upon entering the party, Johns remarked that, "Beer and whiskey containers were knee deep." He goes on to say that "There were about 150 persons there, most of them servicemen from the Olathe navy base."

The two investigators left the party and drove to Gardner to find a phone. Johns called the Johnson County Sheriff's office, and identified himself, and asked for back up to make the raid. He spoke to six dispatchers in the process and multiple deputies, but they all reported that they'd have to have the Sheriff's permission before doing anything. Finally, he reached Norman F. Williams, the Sheriff himself, who refused to help. "He said he was not coming out there to Gardner" Johns later reported, and that the Sheriff said it was all political, anyway. Frustrated, Johns ascended the chain-of-command and phoned Topeka. He reached the state attorney general, Harold Fatzer, and reported the insubordination. The Attorney General called the Sheriff who reluctantly ordered the raid. But the delay had cost the investigators three hours during which approximately 50 men and two strip-tease dancers had left the party.

Confiscated that night were three poker tables, a dice table and two blackjack tables along with booze, cards, dice and poker chips. 100 or so men were rounded up for questioning but later released, with only six men arrested. One of the arrested men was Matthes, the resort operator, bloodied from taking a blow to the mouth.

Eugene Hackler, attorney for Matthes, said that he was considering bringing legal action against Sheriff Williams, whose attack on Mathes was allegedly "without provocation." Matthes, who was charged with possession of gambling equipment, possession of intoxicating beverages, resisting arrest and interfering with an officer performing his duty, had lost three teeth in the scuffle.

Also confiscated that evening were several cigar boxes each containing more than $400 in cash taken from the tables. Evidently, they were the V.F.W.'s cut of the gambling proceeds.

In a later interview, Sheriff Williams said that the Gardner Lake Resort had long been considered a "trouble spot" but that the county had not interfered since it was owned by the city of Gardner. But he attributed his delayed response due to confusion resulting from Johns not properly identifying himself. Williams defended that raid preparations had been initiated immediately and that delays were a result of not having adequate time to prepare.

On September 8th, Sheriff Williams and county attorney James Brady were directed by the state attorney general to report to him on September 23rd in regard to their lack of co-operation, something the Sheriff denied. After their meeting had transpired, the papers reported that they had mended their rift and that the whole issue had been a misunderstanding.

The next day, Ralph E. Roe, 36, commander of the Olathe VFW, was arrested on felony charges for operating a gambling operation. He was released on a $500 bond. His job as a construction worker employed at the courthouse made him an easy apprehension.

On September 30th, a temporary injunction requested by John J. Gardner, a Johnson County assistant attorney, was granted by Judge Earl O'Connor to close the Gardner Lake Resort awaiting hearings seeking a permanent order.

Looking Back

The Kansas City Times reported in their August 18, 1956 issue that Marion L. Matthes (spelled 'Mathes' in *The Gardner News*), former operator of the Gardner Lake Resort, was suing the Johnson County Sheriff, Norman F Williams, for $28,130 for his personal injuries and punitive damages resulting from the blow to his face that resulted in the loss of his teeth. But the bigger loss was to the Gardner community whose kids were denied their roller rink, juke joint and teen town when the building was padlocked indefinitely.

Now, fast-forward 65 years to August 15, 2020, when the author was attending a fund-raiser at the Olathe VFW. During a casual conversation with a distinguished Korean veteran from the area, I happened to mention the incident. As we were discussing the colorful event, I commented on the Sheriff's reluctance to raid the party and speculated on the reasons. He looked at me with a sly smile and said, "I'm sure it had nothing to do with the fact that the Sheriff's son was working the door that night." With surprise I asked, "How do you know this?" The gentleman, Ross Seals, chuckled and said, "I was there."

On March 1, 1956, the Gardner Lake Resort fell into the management of Jess Baird, 1st Lt., USMC and W.V. 'Scotty' Noble, Lt. USMC. The two men launched a complete remodeling of the interior of the building, while the latter of the two also managed the bathing beach.

Children Die in Fire on Lake Road 5

On February 16, 1955, a tragedy touched the Gardner Lake Resort when a fire claimed the lives of the young children belonging to two part-time employees. Peter and Julie "Jutta" La Mirande were working to redecorate the "tavern" when a fire broke out at their cabin located one-half block north of the resort on Lake Road 5. Peter Jr, 3, and his sister Linda Joy, 22 months, were alone in their 3-room cabin around 4:30 pm when the fire was first noticed. Although Peter, Sr "Pete" fought valiantly to rescue the children, he was beaten back by the flames. Firemen from both the Olathe Naval Air Station and Edgerton were not able to extinguish the blaze. The little girl's remains were later found in a charred crib, while the three-year-old was found huddled in the area where there had previously been a closet. The hysterical mother, five months pregnant with a third child, was taken to the naval station hospital for treatment.

Evidently, Pete La Mirande was employed part time at the resort club house as a laborer. He had finished painting and was laying linoleum while his wife was chatting with Mrs. Beryl Pitts, a waitress. She mentioned to Pitts that she was going to go check on the children, again. Moments later she burst into the resort screaming that the house was on fire and to call the fire department.

"While I was talking to the operator, Jutta tried to take the telephone receiver away from me in her hurry to get the fire department. Then she became hysterical." Stated Pitts to a reporter of the *Kansas City Times* in the aftermath.

The cause of the blaze was never determined due to the complete destruction of the property, however, it was believed to have been ignited by faulty wiring.

La Mirande was Airman First Class in the 2472nd air reserve unit stationed at the Olathe Naval Air Station. He had recently returned from a tour of duty in London, England, where he met and married Jutta Reis in 1951. Soon after, the children were born in England. Originally from Bend, Oregon, La Mirande settled his young family at Gardner Lake to be close to his unit.

The La Mirande union did not survive the horrific event, and they later divorced.

Their grand opening was Saturday night, March 31, with music and dancing provided by the Don Shipman Quintet. They offered free registration for a drawing held that night. The March 29 edition of the paper featured a large ad for the event and referred to the venue as the 'Gardner Lake Resort Club.' The two managers expanded their promotion of the club with small ads appearing in the *Kansas City Times* as well. Taking it up a notch still, the managers touted, in one of their weekly ads, that they had 'Dub Jordan and His Bar J Ranch Boys' to entertain in addition to 'Bill Wimberly and His Ozark Jubilee Troop.' Reservations were cash in advance only. In May of 1956, the resort adopted a new tag line. They were "Your Country Club in the Country," featuring the music of 'John Dillinger and his Orchestra.' The cover charge was .75 cents. In August of that year, the managers adopted a new moniker for the club. Their display ads referred to the resort clubhouse as 'Lakeside Country Club.' On Friday night, August 3, they featured Al Flores and his seven-piece orchestra with a vocalist out front. Ladies' admission was half price.

The apex of the two Marines' efforts occurred in the fall of 1956 when the local paper contained three large display ads, in their issue on September 27, that boasted of "our beautiful Knotty Pine (Private) Dining Room." They served five different cuts of grade A charcoal-broiled steaks, ham sandwiches, chili (plain or with beans) and finally, tocas with French fries. (The last item may have been 'tacos'… the paper was in dire need of a proofreader.) A message to their patrons stated, "Remember, Folks, Good Food is not Cheap and Cheap Food is not Good." Dancing at the Lakeside Country Club included moves to an orchestra, square dancing, swing dancing and of course, rock and roll. The performers were equally diverse from night to night.

Like the bathing beach, Scotty's Lakeside Country Club may have been a seasonal operation. Their last ad appeared in late October 1956. No mention of the club was made again until a display ad appeared in the paper announcing the "Season's Grand Opening," on April 4, 1957, with the music of 'Lester Harding's All-Star Dixieland Band.'

Sadly, on April 11, just a week later, their last ad appeared touting the nationally known master of ceremonies and comedian, Mike Caldwell, accompanied by Judy Conrad and his orchestra. Then, that was it.

GARDNER LAKE RESORT CLUBHOUSE

Noble received orders of a transfer away from ONAS. Upon his departure in December 1957, Ruby Smith assumed the management at the resort. Gone from the paper were the sweeping ads announcing menu specials and headliner entertainment. What eventually happened to W.V. "Scotty" Noble is unknown. But what is known is that nobody ever promoted the venue harder during the Gardner Lake Resort's short history than Scotty.

The local paper reported on February 12, 1959, that Mr. and Mrs. Ray Miller of Olathe purchased the Gardner Lake Resort to convert it to a roller rink, again. Their intentions were to remodel and reopen the building "for the convenience of their patrons" with a snack bar and soft drinks. One week later, on February 19, *The Gardner News* reported that it was sold to W. R. and Nellie Churchman of Edgerton, who also owned a cabin on Lake Road 5. They go on to say, "The City Council felt that the resort had been a long-time burden to the city as income from the property did not warrant the city maintaining the property and it was felt that the city should not be in the rental business." As a final blow, they said, "After the last operator of the resort had settled with the city it was decided to dispose of the property." This was confirmed by Ordinance 745, signed into law on March 11, 1959, which provided for the sale of a considerable amount of property at the lake owned by the city, including the Gardner Lake Resort clubhouse, to the Churchman family for $18,500. A review of Gardner's financial reports during the resort years did not support the claim that the rental business was not profitable. Nonetheless, the gavel dropped, and Ordinance 745 was signed into law.

SCOTTY'S Lakeside Country Club

presents

The nationally known MC and Comedian

MIKE CALDWELL

Accompanied by Judy Conrad and His Orchestra

Saturday Night, April 13th

FLOOR SHOW
11:00 P.M.

Ladies Night -- Half Price

Door Prize

GARDNER, KANSAS

The Gardner News, April 11, 1957
Operators like Scotty Noble made a valiant effort to build a successful business at the Gardner Lake Resort clubhouse. He and business partner, Jess Baird, brought in headliner entertainment and offered an upscale menu. This was their last ad before Scotty, a Marine based at ONAS, was transferred out of this area. (Image courtesy of *The Gardner News*)

Looking Back

April 3, 1959 was set as the grand opening of the skating rink. The paper credits Mr. and Mrs. Miller for their exhaustive work on the reinvention of the venue, which suggested, contrary to the early announcement by the paper, that they were actually the managers. A large display ad in the local paper on March 9 goes to great lengths to distance the skating rink from its former identity. The ad invited parents to come and see that they "are operating a clean and respectable place." The promoters add, "Your children will be in good hands while they are skating with us." Evidently, there had been doubt.

During the subsequent remodeling, hardwood maple floorboards covered old pine and formed a perfect surface for roller skating, and the resort attracted a new crowd of younger people. Shirley Bruce Brown VanArsdale, whose family had purchased the furniture store and funeral home in Gardner the previous decade, recalled the skaters stomping the floor to the beat of the popular music of the time. The skates made a thunderous noise.

In the evenings the place transformed from a roller rink to a juke joint adored by young adults, including Irene Eastland Peer, who remembers dancing there. Long-time Gardner resident, Mary Pritchard, recalls dancing there as well.

In December 1959, the transformation was complete. The December 10 paper said that the Millers were no longer the operators at club house, and that the roller rink was being transformed exclusively to a dance pavilion under new management. "They played two-step country music, and it was always packed," Pritchard said. It was a popular venue for special events. Pritchard held her wedding pre-party there in 1961, which was obviously a very special event. Large display ads, which first appeared in late March 1961, boasted

The Gardner News, March 25, 1959
The Gardner Lake Resort clubhouse gasps its last breath as a roller rink. The promoters went to great efforts to distance the clubhouse from its dubious reputation under previous managers. (Image courtesy of *The Gardner News*)

Gardner Lake Resort Clubhouse

that live performances by Standel's Band, Gordon Elliott and His Orchestra, Dewey Richardson's Orchestra, Harvey Boyd's Band and 'The Ambers' were among the headliners. Charlie Freund, Lake Road 4 resident and future lake patrolman, also played in a band there with Smitty Allenbrand. He recalls watching Navy fist fights in progress, to the tune of "Johnny B. Goode." The club was open Tuesdays through Saturdays with live music on all but two nights.

The club didn't open in 1962 but sat vacant instead. Sadly, on May 8 of that year the 25-year-old clubhouse building was destroyed by fire. *Olathe News*, in their May 9 edition, reported that the 2:00 am fire was of an undetermined origin. At the time, it was leased by Lyle Krough of Butler, Missouri, who ran a chain of similar establishments. The fire loss was estimated at $30,000 on the high side. The Gardner police told the Olathe reporter that the club had been a troubled spot up until about two years prior. Afterall, there had only been one knife fight reported since that time. The Gardner city clerk, James Y. Hayes, remarked that the fire appeared to be suspicious. A county deputy sheriff patrolled Lake Road 5 just thirty minutes prior to the fire, and it seemed unlikely that it could have accelerated that quickly, in his opinion. Hayes went on to speculate that it was a device like a 'Molotov Cocktail' that probably started it. Firefighters were sent from Gardner, Edgerton and the Naval Air Station to control the blaze, but their efforts were curtailed by the lack of a source of water. Trucks were required to load water from the water plant below the dam. Ross Bryan remembers the event sadly as he had finally become of age to start enjoying the resort's night life.

Today, all that remains, besides memories, is the original footprint of the foundation visible among the dormant grass of winter. The impression can be seen on the south end of the circle drive at the west 157th Street entrance to Lake Road 5.

Local resident, Kenny Moll, believes that the decline of the resort clubhouse was the result of the strong military presences at the "beer joint." Glenn Bonar, who remembers sitting outside and listening to the music when he was still underage, also remembers a fight that broke out involving the band. According to Bonar, the musicians were breaking their instruments over the heads of the agitators. Fisticuffs were not uncommon at the club during the 1950's.

Chapter 13
KEEPING THE PEACE

On May 8, 1940, *The Gardner Gazette* published Ordinance 518 establishing the lake rules and regulations. The full-page publication outlined the fees and permit structures for boating, fishing and swimming at the new lake. Fishing limits were defined, and gasoline-powered boats were restricted to official patrol purposes only. The city made provisions for hiring up to three lake patrolmen, and immediately filled the positions. The patrolmen were provided with a boat with a motor "with such horsepower as to permit rapid patrolling." At the time, the only powered boats were for fishing, and they were limited to a three-horsepower motor. The patrol boat was equipped with a siren and light. The patrolmen, also referred to as "caretakers," were permitted to operate, for their own profit, the boat rental concession and beach house as part of their compensation.

Lake Road 5 summer resident, Karla Kuchemeister, recalls the lake patrolman in the 1950's. "A kindly older man in overalls" would pick the young girl up and take her on his rounds of the lake. "He shared his onion and butter sandwiches with me," Kuchemeister recalls warmly. Together they would fish.

In 1952, the lake patrolman was Thomas Jefferson "Jeff" Edemann. The Edemann family moved to the caretaker's cottage with two daughters, Laura and Darlene. The furnished home, located near the beach house, was part of Edemann's compensation. It had electricity and running water, by virtue of a hand pump in the kitchen, which accessed the water captured in a cistern.

The family used an outhouse for their sanitary needs. The tiny living room had a rock fireplace, as daughter Darlene Edemann Prier recalled in a 2020 interview. It was located where Gardner Road now runs in front of 15655 Lake Road 4. Ironically, that latter address is where Darlene lived as an adult.

During the day, Edemann patrolled the lake in an aluminum boat with his black cocker spaniel. Prier's older sister, Laura Edemann McKaig, recalled the time her father laid in hiding to catch an Air Force officer from ONAS, who snuck out and fished without a license. He busted Gary Prier, Darlene's boyfriend, who later became his son-in-law. The family had a big laugh over that, although patrolman Edemann was all business about his responsibilities.

Patrolman Edemann
Lake patrolman Thomas Jefferson "Jeff" Edemann as he appeared on a typical duty day. He was a stickler for the rules, but very unpretentious in his delivery of the law. (Photo courtesy of the Cyndy Prier family archives)

Looking Back

Edemann served the lake for the three years prior to his untimely death on July 21, 1955, at the age of 60. The Edemann family left the caretaker's house and moved to Olathe in September of that year.

In early 1958, Paul R. Aver of Olathe replaced Edemann as lake patrolman and caretaker, but that was short-termed. Later in the year, Aver was replaced by Joe Burton.

During 1959, Joe Burton established, or perpetuated, a retail business at the caretaker's residence on the east side of the lake. A large ad appeared in *The Gardner News* on May 28 promoting the sale of fishing tackle, rods and reels, and bait. The retail shop offered Father's Day specials, which suggested that the number of anglers visiting the lake must have been considerable. After all, during that time, the lake had only twenty-eight permanent residences. Referred to more often as a 'custodian' than patrolman, Burton was praised for his brush collecting and trash pick-up rather than his law enforcement verve. In the August 6, 1959, edition of *The Gardner News*, there was mention that the lake patrolman had four assistants. But during the decade of the 1950s, the population of Gardner tripled, so it stands to reason that the traffic on the lake would have as well. The job was anything but lucrative by today's standards, but it afforded Burton a new Renault Dauphine, as reported in the news on June 2, 1960.

In 1961, Paul McDaniels assumed the role as lake patrolman. The paper reports in November of that year that he injured his foot burning brush. His departure was soon after, but that appears to be unrelated to his burn.

At the end of 1961, Charlie Freund became the lake patrolman who replaced McDaniels. Charlie recalls the job as being all-encompassing and more than full-time. He and wife Linda, and new baby Mike, lived in the caretaker's house that was still provided. From there, the two of them sold fishing licenses, tackle and bait from a minnow tank. When Charlie wasn't patrolling, he was tasked with maintaining all the parks that surrounded the lake, trimming weeds and picking up trash. He remembers cleaning out the spillway of encroaching brush and piling a mountain of branches. And if that weren't enough, he filled in for the only police officer Gardner had when the officer needed a day off or took vacation. Interestingly, Freund also played in a band at the Gardner Lake Resort in the evenings when he was not needed to patrol the lake.

KEEPING THE PEACE

Often a victim of ridicule for his ample girth, Rolla Daggs patrolled the lake in the late 1960's and early 1970's. He came down hard on the kids who failed to show respect for his authority. Ed Hayes recalls witnessing an occasion when Daggs' small run-about was surrounded by kids who rocked the boat violently. In a panic, Daggs got free and sped from the scene, red-faced, among howls of laughter. Hayes, a Lake Road 10 resident and a deputy at the Johnson County Sherrif's Office, became Daggs' confidant. Hayes, with his background in law enforcement, recalls counseling the portly man on how to diplomatically handle such situations. Hayes, in a phone interview on June 27, 2022, said that his overwhelming feeling towards Daggs was that of pity. Daggs was not trained for the position and was frustrated that he could not command the respect that he and the position deserved. Sadly, even the adults joined in the jeering, according to Hayes. It was hard to watch.

Walt Bickley spent summers at the lake in the late 1960's, and as a young boy, swam from sunup to sundown. His daily routine included swimming the length of the dam from Lake Road 1 to the spillway and back, which was observed by Daggs. Bickley recalls Daggs, in his sweat-soaked safari attire, pulling his sidearm and laying a bead on the boy's head. "You are in a heap of trouble" were Daggs' words, according to Bickley, who was then forced to swim home at gun point. Poncho Ruiz, long-time resident of Lake Road 10, said that Daggs was never seen without his .45 caliber sidearm.

Boys on Hydroplanes
Bob Stockmyer, Larry Keegan, and friends created a bit of mischief around the lake on their homemade hydroplanes, much to the chagrin of patrolman Rolla Daggs. Ironically, years later, Larry would end up filling in as lake patrolman when his father, Phil, was unavailable for duty. (Photo courtesy of the Larry Keegan family archives)

Looking Back

Denise Churchwell Campanella remembers patrolman Daggs quite differently. She was very fond of the big man, who was also her neighbor at the lake. "He was nothing but nice to me," she recalls. They often went fishing together. She goes on to say, "His boat looked like a patrol boat, and he looked like an official patrolman." She remembers that his boat might have had a siren. "He was a stickler for safety."

After the untimely death of Rolla Daggs in August 1976, Phil Keegan assumed that position, but handled his responsibilities quite differently. Ununiformed and unarmed, he primarily chased down unpermitted fishermen. Rather than writing a ticket, Keegan would sell them a license on the spot.

Lake resident since 1966, Linda Sladish recalls antagonizing Daggs, but said the kids responded quite differently to Keegan. She commented "When he saw us kids swimming where we shouldn't, he (Keegan) would come by and just talk with us. Never mentioned the rules, got to know us kids and we started obeying the rule(s). He was an amazing guy."

Patrolman Keegan
Lake patrolman Phil Keegan was very popular around the lake. He is seen here in his patrolman uniform provided by the city, complete with a badge. (Photo courtesy of the Larry Keegan family archives)

KEEPING THE PEACE

When he was unavailable to perform his duties, Keegan's son, Larry, would assume those responsibilities after work in the evenings. Ironically, Larry was one of several boys who tormented Daggs by speeding around on hydroplane boats with his friend, Bob Stockmyer, son and grandson of two of the original lake project organizers, during the 1960's.

In the early 1980's, the lake had its first and only patrolwoman in Donna Stewart Wiliker, who remembers the job paying $250 a month. She also recalls a serious run-in with a particularly ornery and fractious boy in his early teens. This boy, who will remain unnamed, would get in the family motorboat and speed around terrorizing other children. When he saw a picnic on the shore, he sped as fast as possible to the shoreline and rolled the boat at the last minute to avoid a crash. He sent families scattering for safety with plates of overturned food. What he was doing was dangerous, and it scared Wiliker. But the boy laughed and moved on to the next innocent victims. Wiliker's phone rang off the wall with complaints from neighbors. The boy lived only two doors down from Wiliker, so she knew well who he was. After one bad incident, she dragged him home and presented the situation to his mother. His mother behaved no better and started arguing, bickering and threatening Wiliker. With no options left, Wiliker called the Gardner police, and they were on the site in just a few minutes, in her support. Not long after that, Wiliker moved from the lake.

Thirty years passed, and she returned for a visit. She attended a Christmas party with old friends and neighbors, and found the boy, now a grown man, there with his mother. Both had changed dramatically, "Even the mother matured," stated Wiliker, who received sincere apologies and it all ended warmly.

One of the last patrolmen was current lake road resident, Scott Burnett, who served for several years during the 1980s. He was hired for the year-round, salaried job by lake advocate, and social page editor, Oma Girsch. Since all Burnett's duties occurred during the summer months, Burnett asked Girsch, "So, what do I do during the winter months?" Her quick answer was, "Well, I wouldn't quit, if I were you." His favorite job was feeding the fish twice a day from the fish feeder located in Pirate's Cove at the time. Six or eight delighted kids filed in his city-provided patrol boat to observe the feeding frenzy. Spotting the huge albino catfish was a special treat for everyone.

Looking Back

Shelby Moore was probably the last patrolman to serve the lake. The City of Gardner continued to provide the position until October 4, 1993, when the City Council voted to place the position into the department of public safety. The state assumed the responsibility of water safety under the Kansas Department of Wildlife, Parks and Tourism. They provide a game warden for those tasks. Although they are rarely seen, the atmosphere at the lake remains peaceful, for the most part.

Gardner Lake Claims Its First Life

It is somewhat remarkable that the lake construction project had no accidental deaths to record. You had hundreds of unskilled workers around megatons of loose rock and heavy equipment. But bruises and scrapes were the order of the day, with an occasion broken bone. A. S. Reece's camp infirmary was usually filled with flu patients.

It was almost twenty years later when the lake claimed its first casualty, and tragically, it was a 16-year-old athlete from Olathe enjoying the early summer weather.

On June 3, 1952, Gary Boyd, a student at Olathe High School, and a member of the football and basketball teams, was swimming near the dock at the bathing beach with his friend, Calvin Leonard and two other buddies. Evidently, about 1:00 pm, the two boys decided to swim across to the east shore and back. Boyd was strong and had completed Red Cross lifesaving tests. He was considered an expert swimmer and was being sought for lifeguarding positions in the area. This should not have been difficult.

On the return run, within about 30 feet of the bathing beach dock, he exclaimed to Leonard, a few feet in the lead, what sounded like "Oh!" and disappeared under the surface. Leonard looked over his shoulder but did not see Boyd. He rushed to the dock, screaming for help, alerted other friends, and they immediately began diving to find the young man. Help was summoned from a nearby cottage. Within 40 minutes, ONAS had deployed 20 lifeguards and divers and the Sheriff's department had sent out a dragline. The search was intense but had to be suspended at nightfall for lack of underwater lighting. The hunt resumed the next morning to no avail. Boyd's parents, Rev. and Mrs. Floyd Boyd, were obviously grief stricken.

The story was so compelling that it was syndicated and picked up by regional papers like the Manhattan Mercury. Everyone waited anxiously, though there was little hope. Finally, rescue efforts were abandoned but a watch was maintained for the victim's body.

On early Sunday morning, June 29th, 26 days later, two fishermen from Shawnee spotted the lifeless remains floating near the spillway. The funeral was held at Rev. Boyd's First Baptist Church in Olathe as the family struggled to recover. Gary now rests in Olathe city cemetery.

Jimmie Lee Mulkey, 7-year old son of Mr. and Mrs. Matt Mulkey of Sunflower Village, was wading in the shallow pool at the bathing beach on Tuesday evening, June 22, 1954. His father had taken him and his brother William, 10, for a car ride around Gardner Lake. The boys had asked to stop at the beach to wade in the shallow water marked by posts. Evidently, Jimmie wandered into the deeper water before his father realized it. Jimmie was found by a swimmer about five minutes later. Attempts by ONAS personnel to resuscitate the boy, with equipment brought by the base, failed. He is buried in the Williamstown, Kansas cemetery.

Unfortunately, that was not the last drowning tragedy. A particularly compelling incident happened on August 27, 1958 when a 13-month old toddler escaped his mother's attention while she was changing the diaper on her 5-day old daughter, Sherrie. Mark Douglas Laaksonen, son of Joan and Wilfred Laaksonen, a radarman stationed at ONAS, crawled down to the dock from their back yard on the west side of the lake.

About 100 personnel were dispatched from the navy air station in addition to volunteer firemen and neighbors and the search was on.

However, it was Mrs. Laaksonen who solved the mystery of the missing child. She stated that, "I looked around the neighbors' houses, then found one of the dogs down by the lake." Their family pet, crouched and whimpering by the dock, had located the lifeless child. Though rushed to the Reece Hospital in Gardner, it was obviously too late, and the boy was pronounced dead.

On Saturday, June 9, 1965, Ronnie Faught, 19, of Olathe, was swimming with friends at the bathing beach. Swimming at the dock with three other friends, the boys noticed Ronnie starting to struggle. The three of them thought he was joking. At one point, one of the boys, Darrell Piettarila, reached out to Ronnie who grabbed his hand briefly, then let go and slipped under the waters. Still believing it was a practical joke, they waited briefly before diving in to locate him. Visibility in the water was limited to two feet due to heavy rains earlier that week. Members of the Johnson County sheriff's search and rescue team located Ronnie's body about an hour and a half later.

Chapter 14
THE PRECARIOUS RELATIONSHIP WITH ONAS

In the 1940s, Gardner's town fathers learned of the Navy's plan to locate a Naval Air Station in the Midwest. It seemed like an odd location for a floating branch of the armed forces, but it was ideal for the large number of student flyers who needed to be trained. With constant fear of foreign invasion, the inland location offered protection and the flat terrain was perfect for the construction of airfields.

The battle commenced between Olathe and Gardner for the location, with city council members from both municipalities rushing to Washington, D.C. to pitch for their venue. The presence of the base would certainly stimulate a town's economy. The availability of water from Gardner Lake and the proximity of nearby Gardner Municipal Airport tipped the scales, and Gardner won out. The site was selected in December 1940. However, Gardner lost the battle for the name, which ended up being Olathe Naval Air Station, or 'Navy Olathe' for short. Although Gardner was certainly closer, a large post office was needed to handle the volume of correspondence, and Olathe was better suited for handling the mail.

The Precarious Relationship with ONAS

The Olathe Naval Air Station (ONAS) was completed and commissioned on October 1, 1942. In January of that year, the city council, in an act of patriotism, decided to give the defense department the raw water from the lake. In addition, they agreed to lease the land below the dam for the construction of a water treatment plant, for a dollar a year. The navy built the treatment plant, and the spillway and grounds were kept pristine by the sailors. Due to fear of sabotage during the war years, guard houses were constructed on both entrances of the dam to prevent public access to the dam and spillway. Glenn Bonar recalls that the officers were kind enough to let him use the guard house as a bus stop shelter in 1945.

Aerial view of the Olathe Naval Air Station
This photo was taken a few weeks prior to the commissioning of ONAS in 1942. It is likely that the presence of the air station changed the trajectory of the lake. In the foreground are the enlisted men's barracks. (Photo courtesy of the Gardner Historical Museum)

Looking Back

Up to that time, the young lake served exclusively for recreation. The weekend inhabitants did use the lake water for their unpotable needs but hauled treated water from town for their weekend consumption. The city was using a series of wells north of town for their treated water supply. But the well water was proving to be inadequate for the growing town, prompting the mayor to encourage conservation. Wells dug around the lake during the WPA years also fell short of the requirements.

The complexion of the lake dramatically changed, due to the proximity of ONAS. As a result of housing shortages, the lake population grew rapidly with new, year-round tenants made up of officers and defense contractors. During that time, 159th Street, previously a meandering dirt farm road to the Harrington homestead, was cut through to connect to Gardner East Road. This facilitated a shorter commute to the base. These lake newcomers required more water still.

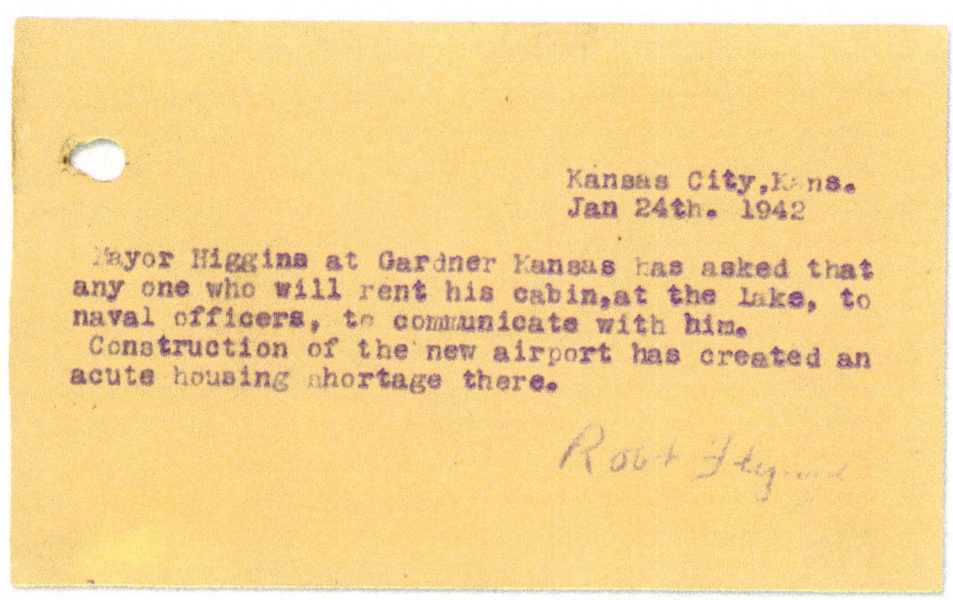

The Mayor's Direct Mailer
Mayor Higgins reached out to property owners at the lake to encourage weekenders to turn their cottages into rentals to ease the housing shortage issues. (Courtesy of the Herb and Helen Klemp family archives)

The Precarious Relationship with ONAS

The appearance of the lake changed as well. In early 1943, when the Navy had control of the lake, they added a foot of concrete to the top of the spillway and raised the water levels as much. This change to the shoreline eliminated large sections of the walking path that encompassed the lake.

Sadly, *The Gardner Gazette* suspended printing due to the death of their senior editor and a paper shortage created by the global conflict. Their last edition appeared on October 21, 1942, and ironically, it included a large advertisement promoting the sale of subscriptions. Evidently, the suspension was abrupt and unplanned. Frank Cramer, co-founder of Cramer Chemical, the town's largest industry, decided to act. He published, at his expense, the monthly *Home Town News,* which first appeared in December 1942. It was designed exclusively for the Gardner servicemen and women now deployed abroad. Not intended as 'hard news', it was filled with gossip, inside jokes and jabs at local citizens. Certainly, it was a morale booster and must have been greatly anticipated by those serving away from home. It was published through April of 1944.

On July 13, 1944, *The Gardner News* emerged, published and edited by H.C. Winkler from Spring Hill. A lake news column reappeared, possibly written by Mrs. John T. Patty, but the tone was restrained compared to her earlier style and flare from the *Gazette* days.

But things changed at the lake. The residents were disconnected soldiers and sailors from distant locales. The new inhabitants rented from cottage owners solicited by the mayor on January 24, 1942, to help ease the housing shortage. Mostly gone from the papers are the familiar names of the Gardner town leaders and socialites who frequented their property at the lake. In a show of patriotic support, or self-preservation, many original cottage owners surrendered their property and never returned.

Looking Back

A letter dated June 24, 1944, from the Gardner Lake Lot Owners Association president Ray R. Michaels pleaded with cottage owners for help. He stated, "Your (GLLOA) officers feel that they should call your attention to an alarming situation which is fast developing around our lake. Many of our cabin owners have rented their cabins to defense workers and military personnel. Some of these tenants are conscientious people who make every effort to keep from throwing trash and garbage around carelessly. The majority of them, however, we are sorry to say, just don't care. Only recently, we were amazed to see great quantities of tin cans and garbage scattered all over our picnic grounds and jammed into the ovens." He goes on to say, "Ask your tenant to burn or bury his garbage. Don't let them throw it into the lake. Many of our people are pumping lake water into their cabins for various uses, and they don't want garbage mixed in it." Michaels also commented on an issue with weeds and brush. He closed the letter with, "In the meantime, your officers are working on a plan of law enforcement which should solve a great number of our problems of law violations around the lake. We hope to have some good news for our members shortly. In the meantime, we ask the increased support of our association. Attend its meetings regularly, pay your dues promptly, and support the aims of your officers. If you see a violation of lake laws occurring before your eyes, speak up fearlessly and tell the offender about it. Your officers are fighting to make Gardner Lake, with its fine potentialities the kind of lake our federal government intended it should be, and we aren't quitting until we have accomplished that objective." The same newsletter laments that they must raise the dues from two dollars to two dollars and fifty cents.

The Precarious Relationship with ONAS

> "Most of you boys have heard of the Olathe Naval Station of Gardner, Kansas. You will recall how it used to be the Gardner base and how we gave our lake so that they could have water."
>
> "Now Olathe has the base and along with it our lake. All we get to do is keep up the park, mow the weeds, keep it stocked with fish, trim the trees and keep the roads in shape…..for Olathe."
>
> **Frank Cramer, Editor**
> *The Home Town News* – **January, 1943**

Now, gone from the local papers were the quaint articles by Mrs. John T. Patty describing a paradise around the sparkling waters dotted by adorable cottages.

Sadly, this episode may have started the divide between the city of Gardner and the lake that some feel still exists today. The City of Gardner seemed emotionally detached for the first time.

Although there is no military presence now, it is woven into the history of the lake, quite literally. According to Karen Barber, when she and John Modic were remodeling their duplex at 15958 Gardner East Road, they found that it had been insulated with shredded WWII uniforms.

A Slippery Situation Between Navy and Lake

In late April of 1952, Clifford Cravens, manager of the Gardner Lake Resort, noticed the presence of an oily film on the lake. At the time, he ran the boat rental concession and sold beer, tackle and fishing licenses. Therefore, it was to him that complaints were registered. He traced the source to the Olathe Naval Air Station by means of a small drainage ditch with low visibility. When it was called to the attention of Capt. James H. Flatley, the commanding officer at the base, a leaking 11,000-gallon tank of aircraft engine lubricant was identified as the source. Evidently, 3,100 gallons of oil had escaped through a leak over the previous few days and had found its way to the lake through the 1.5-mile drainage ditch.

Immediately, eight sailors were dispatched to the lake with burlap bags to work in shifts of eight hours to mop up the mess. Most of the oil was still in the ditch which was then dammed off and the oil ignited.

Cravens threatened to sue the Federal Government, and the Universal Construction Company, who built the tank, for $3,000 in damages and lost revenues. His customers were complaining that the oil had ruined their tackle and clothing, and that the situation would impact their fishing success.

In an effort to assess the damage, the Navy dispatched G.W. Akers, a ship's cook, and his wife Myrtle. With fishing poles in hand, they reported catching seventy-two blue gill and crappie that evening. The next night, Akers took a fishing buddy, Tech Sargent Jack Colberg of the Air Force unit stationed at ONAS, to the lake with his wife, Linda. Between them they caught another forty fish. The following day, Akers and Colberg, both fly fishing and bait casting, caught another forty-two blue gill and crappie, from six inches to eleven inches in length, in two and a half hours. They also caught bass, but they were too young so they returned them to the water.

The Navy men hypothesized that the oil film killed off the mosquito and other insect larva, cutting down the food supply and causing the fish to go hungry. They quipped that, by July, the fish will be so hungry they will jump into the boat. No bait will be needed.

Chapter 15
HARVESTING THE LAKE

In August 1947, the U.S. Navy permitted the City of Gardner to tap into their water treatment plant below the dam to resolve the shortage issue for the town. A four-inch water main was connected to the Navy's pumping station, and on August 13, Gardner city residents were guaranteed an endless supply of water, or so they thought, from Gardner Lake. However, it was easy to underestimate the Navy's water requirements, which averaged 104 million gallons a year. The limited supply of water became critical during dry spells.

In 1953, Gardner's water boost pump was down for repair. Gardner citizens experienced low water pressure, but the outlying houses on city water, mostly farms, were getting none. To curtail the situation, the ONAS water plant below the dam was selling water to Gardner, who, in turn, sold it to the farmers. However, it had to be hauled by truck. This had been going on for several weeks when *The Gardner News* broke the story on May 3, 1953.

Exacerbating the situation, the City of Gardner started selling water to other neighboring communities as well. In November 1953, officials from Gardner, the ONAS and Olathe sat down to resolve the issue. The prolonged drought made Olathe Lake, the city reservoir, inadequate to meet the needs of that growing town. Officials agreed that the Gardner Lake water would be sold to Olathe until a point in which the ONAS and Gardner's supply was threatened. On 151st Street, a convoy of trucks collected water from the plant below the dam and transported it to Olathe. Water was rolling out steadily between 6:00 am to 7:00 pm.

Looking Back

Even the *Great Bend Tribune* picked up the story. On February 8, 1954, they reported that Olathe had a water line break which caused the loss of 10,000 gallons. It accumulated in the basement of a local hotel. The burden on Garden Lake was now greater.

FEB 1954

The Breitensteins on Pirate's Cove in 1954
The mid 1950's presented a challenging situation for the lake due to high temperatures and chronic drought. The Cities of Gardner, Olathe, and other neighboring communities, turned to Gardner Lake for their water supply. This coupled with unexpected high utilization by ONAS brought about extremely low water levels. The situation prevailed in 1954 and 1955. (Photo courtesy of the Anne Breitenstein Sooter family archives)

Harvesting the Lake

Looking south at Pirate's Cove
This photo was taken during the water crisis of 1954. (Photo courtesy of the Anne Breitenstein Sooter family archives)

The Gardner News edition on March 18, 1954, reported that dust bowl conditions prevailed. High winds and dry conditions created a blowing dust situation that reduced visibilities to zero in places. Highway accidents were reported where motorists weren't proceeding cautiously.

In July 1954, Gardner placed water restrictions on residents' water usage. The paper was quick to point out that the supply wasn't the issue, it was the limitations of the four-inch pipe previously installed to carry Gardner Lake water from ONAS to Gardner's water plant. However, they also eliminated the sale of water by the truckload except for domestic usage around Gardner, and that was limited to 500 gallons a load. The article said that plans were being made for a larger water line between ONAS and Gardner.

That year, the heat was brutal with records being broken every day. In mid-July, Olathe recorded temperatures of 114 degrees and Ottawa at 117. Crops were stressed and people were suffering. On July 15, members of the city council met to discuss the installation of a larger supply line from ONAS.

Lake residents were alarmed. Docks were left marooned in a sea of mud and lake dweller's water supply lines laid exposed on the silt bed. Helpless lake residents watched as their shoreline grew and their lake shrank. The worst of these years was in 1954, but the issue would continue for years.

Brooding over the situation, the Gardner City Council proposed a special election for May 28, 1955 to present a bond issue to raise the money to fix the water issue once and for all. Their answer was a larger, eight-inch supply line from ONAS' water plant below the dam to increase the flow provided by the lake. The estimated cost was $132,000. Ordinance 650 proposed a $100,000 general obligation bond with $32,000 made up by the sale of waterworks revenue bonds. In addition to the larger supply line, the ordinance provided for the enlargement and improvement of the water treatment facility. The proposal was signed by Mayor Shelby Jones, former superintendent of the lake construction project.

The issue passed by a vast majority of voters, numbering eighty-seven, with only four votes in opposition. Bear in mind, the population of the city was only 1000 at the time.

Two months later, in July, a notice from the mayor appeared in the paper announcing that bulk water could again be purchased below the dam, and again a convoy hauled off the precious commodity.

The water crisis eased slightly in 1956, with fewer references to the shortages in the local paper. However, on March 14, 1957, a front-page article in *The Gardner News* announced that restrictions were placed on water usage due to previous years of drought. The paper said, "If rigid conservation of water is not immediately practiced, it may be necessary to resort to the establishment of water hours in the very near future."

The Spring of 1957 proved to be a wet one. In June, a front-page headline reads, "GARDNER LAKE AGAIN RUNS OVER SPILLWAY." It was the first time since 1951 that the lake was full. In the June 26 edition, Charla Wilson wrote, "I can't remember seeing the water in Gardner Lake so high in the eighteen years that we have been there."

In early 1959, the new water plant was complete and operational below the dam. Instead of tapping the treated water from the Navy's plant, Gardner was now independently taking the water. Already 3,000,000 gallons were consumed. The State Board of Health indicated that the plant was "producing top quality water."

Kids swimming off South Gardner Place with Gardner East Road in background.
Photo taken in 1961. (Courtesy Mary Gill Broski family archives)

Chig's Water War

In 1964 a conflict erupted with Gardner Mayor Howard "Chig" Lawrence that earned national attention. A $14.0M project had been approved by Congress to construct Hillsdale Lake as a replacement source of water, but the funds had yet to be appropriated by the Federal Government. Lawrence's tireless efforts to get attention to the issue led him several times to Washington D.C. to appeal to everyone from the POTUS down, but it was to no avail. When he approached the Army Corp of Engineers, the Kansas State Board of Water Resources, the Bureau of Reclamation, the Bureau of the Budgets, as well as the state lawmakers, the response was just one of sympathy. To gain attention to the issue, Lawrence, a WWII Navy veteran himself, would cut the water off to ONAS; or at least say he was going to cut it off.

Now, you would think that the mayor of Gardner, a town of 1,847 citizens, would know who owned the equipment below the dam that treated and pumped that water. It wasn't the City of Gardner. So, either Lawrence wasn't very smart, or like most believe, he was smart like a fox.

When the commanding officer at the air station, Capt. Thomas L. Andrews, heard the threat, he was astonished. He said he would believe it if they were in Hong Kong, or somewhere else in Red China, but not in the heart of the nation. But the threat found legs, and the national media picked up the story. And evidently, the stunt worked because the Hillsdale Lake Association was founded and Lawrence served as its president from 1964 until 1969. The rest is history, and finally there was plenty of water to go around.

PART III
THE FIRST EIGHTEEN YEARS

Herbie Klemp is perched by his mother on the window sill of their stone cottage on Lake Road 8.
This photo was taken in July of 1940 while the cottage was under construction."
Photo courtesy of the Helen and Herb Klemp family archives.

Looking Back

The following is an article that appeared in *The Gardner News* on June 27, 1957. It was written by Charla Hudler Wilson and is included here in its entirety. With her husband, F. Condry Wilson, the couple built a cottage on Lake Road 11 in 1939, establishing them as some of the earliest inhabitants. The cottage, affectionately known as "Red Shutters", was demolished in 2021. If still there, the address would be 29380 W. 153rd Terrace. This article is Charla's recollections of the changes that had occurred over the previous 18 years at Gardner Lake.

> Those who built Gardner Lake in its early youth will remember the main body of water in the old river bed with a trickle of water reaching out into the northeast arm. Many were skeptical of the water's ever reaching its present height because the filling of the lake was a very slow process. However the beach, with its attractive bathhouse, the picnic grounds with their ovens, picnic tables and even an incinerator for complete trash disposal, newly drilled wells and a rock walk around the lake, all furnished by the government, were very encouraging to those who wanted to enjoy the privileges of a weekend resort long before their cabins were completed. It wasn't uncommon to see a wife wearing a carpenter's apron with nails in the pocket and a hammer in her hand, helping her husband finish just enough of the cabin to insure a good roof over their heads so they could move in and complete the interior. Getting the necessary furniture out to the lake from the city was always a chore and many items were traded- such as refrigerators for electric stoves. Before electricity was brought to some parts of the lake, we used a "smelly" coal oil stove and a coal oil lamp with a mantle for brighter light, which we were fortunate enough to find.
>
> There were very few trees about the lake except on the south side of the northeast arm and east of Lookout Point and the south end. It was truly amazing to see many small trees appear and grow into beautiful shade that now surround the lake, due to the rise in the water table as the lake water rose.

THE FIRST EIGHTEEN YEARS

Probably because of our dependence upon one another, it seemed very easy to become acquainted. Soon an organization was formed which met one a month, a social period following the meetings. Group picnics were planned and one or two big parties a season were held at the beach for parents and children. There were games and swimming races and a big spread of picnic suppers. As I interview people around the lake I am often asked why we aren't having something of this sort now, especially by the old timers (not in years but in length of time at the lake). There probably is no reason. Of course there are more people here now, but that should only add to the volume of good times.

If there was enough interest perhaps we could eventually have many of our hopes fulfilled-drinking water, even sewers and gas but, most of all a sanitary lake.

Many have asked about the lack of walk around the lake now. Originally the government constructed a rock walk slightly above the water's point. Later, (if I remember correctly-when the naval base needed water) it was deemed necessary to increase the volume and the spillway was raised. The water then covered part of the walk and in other places washed away the earth beneath until the rocks fell in. This explanation may also answer the many questions as to why there seems to be a fringe of large rocks right below the water's edge in many places.

If the lot owners at the lake have any pressing questions or interesting information about the lake, send them to Mrs. F. C. Wilson, Lake Road 11, Gardner Kansas. Through the interviews or experience at the lake it may be possible to unearth the answers.

Chapter 16
THE FIRST FAMILIES

With almost nine decades on Lake Road 8, Herb Klemp should be recognized as having the longest tenure at the lake. It started when Herb's German immigrant parents, Heinrich "Heinie" and Wilhelmina "Mimi," became interested in purchasing a lake lot. They adopted Kansas City, Kansas, as their hometown, and KCK's Chamber of Commerce sold lots to support Gardner's effort to build the lake. Heinie, along with his friend and neighboring KCK businessman, Phillip Volz, and wife Bertha, agreed to purchase lots at the same time and become neighbors. When their lottery numbers were called on Sunday, April 18, 1937, they scrambled to Lake Road 8 and staked out adjacent lots with a breathtaking view of the lake to their southwest, and a beautiful park in their back yards.

By 1940, when Herb was just a baby, the Klemps and Volzs each completed sturdy, rustic-style, stone-and-frame structures that still stand side-by-side today. Herb remembers when they hauled drinking water from home and used self-treated lake water for other kitchen and bathing needs. Most summer weekends were spent on the water. The cottages were closed for the winter months.

Herb met his lovely wife, Helen Grove, on a blind date in 1958 when she was only 16. Herb, who was 19 at the time, had just returned from a year in California. Eventually, Helen joined the ranks of TWA as a flight attendant and became a moving target for Herb, so their dating was on and off for years.

The First Families

But they finally married in 1964, and Helen also became enchanted with the Gardner Lake life.

Three daughters, Brenda, Melissa and Kathryn, followed soon, and they, too, had lake water in their veins. In 1989, they built a handsome house on the adjacent lots to the northwest and incorporated the original cottage for a beautiful and nostalgic effect. That became, and remains, their full-time residence. Both Herb and Helen have been stalwart supporters as volunteers on the Gardner Lake Association. Herb was the president of GLA in the early 1990's, and Helen published the lake newsletters.

The Klemp Family
Heinie, Herbie and Mimi Klemp at their Lake Road 8 house they built in 1940. This photo was taken Easter morning in 1944. (Photo courtesy of the Herb and Helen Klemp family archives)

When the Volz family left the lake in the 1950's, they rented their cottage to a couple named Chapman. He was stationed at the Olathe Naval Air Station, like so many other lake residents at the time. In the early 1990's, the Klemps purchased the Volz cottage and incorporated it in their handsome spread on the hilltop. However, the Volz family did not become strangers to the lake. With warm memories of sunny weekends with her family, Karen Rohner Scott, granddaughter of Phillip and Bertha Volz, brought her husband to the lake in 2014. They found their current home on Lake Road 12 and are keeping their bloodline established on the water.

"Haderway" and "Dunwanderin"

With all the joy provided by a cottage on the lake, it seemed only natural that these beloved structures would take on a persona of their own. Soon after construction, many of the quaint cabins were bestowed clever names.

This is the case with *"Haderway,"* one of the lake first retreats and the joy of Charles and Bess Cramer in the late '30's. Rumor had it that Bess wasn't fully on board for the move from their home in Gardner. However, when she laid her eyes on the sunny point on the south shore of Pirate's Cove, where Lake Road 10 meets Lake Road 11, she told her husband that the only way she'd agree to his new ambition would be if it were located on that point. Well, she had her way, and the point and the cottage came to be known as *Haderway*. Gatherings were weekly during the warm months at *Haderway*. In the early 1950s, C.D. Hansen came to own the property and renamed it *Holiday Point*. However, in 1957, Hanson moved two doors south to *Happy Hours* and the Russel Utz family took possession of *Holiday Point* and now called their house *Blue Haven*. Sadly, it was abandoned and demolished decades later.

De Lights is another great example of a cabin moniker, and the ending to this story is much happier. Evidently, the employees club at the Kansas City Power and Light Company scored a couple lots on the southeast side of the lake. This may have been the result of bartering for electrical service by the Gardner Lake Corporation, as there was a lot of that going on at the time. The cabin the employees built came to be known as *De Lights*, for obvious reasons. Tastefully enlarged, it is now the beautiful home at 15964 Gardner East Road. During a recent remodeling, the owners reported that they found, inlayed in the original floor, decorative images of the card suites. Playing bridge was a favorite pastime during the 1940's and 50's.

The Double Cottage, located at 16010 Gardner East Road, was built as a duplex prior to 1941, possibly by a gentleman named Robert Gray. In August of 1944 *The Gardner News* reported that he painted it 'cadet blue'. In later years, the Gardner Lake Corporation treasurer, Howard Bigelow, made his full-time home in the south unit. During that time, the north unit was the weekend getaway for Lorene Higgins and family.

Another early cottage, that was lovingly named, was *Dunwanderin*. Although the location is unknown, it was the retreat of the Ross Page family of Gardner in the late '30s.

The R.S. Havely family of Kansas City, Kansas built *Shady Rest* in 1941 according to *The Gardner Gazette.* The Spencer family had *Weez Anne* for a weekend getaway while the Spring Hill family of V.C. Zeigler enjoyed *Zigmoor.*

The Francis Spencer family named their cabin *Week-Am* and *Reesewood* was the retreat of the R.M. Reeser family.

Meanwhile, the John Bishop family relaxed at *The Duckling* (or *Duck In*) and the R.S. Nelson family at *Lake Haven*. Somewhere in Block 1 was the cottage of E.A. Teepan known as *The Oriole*. Lt. and Mrs. D. Miller's *Dusty Miller's* and somewhere on the lake was a *Sanghira*. In later years, on Lake Road 14, the Henderson family bonded at *Boon Docks*, making it their home from 1962 to 1982. *The Oars* was a cottage occupied by two Waves from the Olathe Naval Air Station. This probably turned out to be the original Breitenstein cottage at 29395 Lake Road 14 as the family acquired their first of many lake houses in the late 1940's. Elsewhere on the lake sat *Woody's Rest* along with the Tallaferro cabin known as, what else, *Tally Ho*.

Interestingly, Lake Roads 9 and 10 were referred to as "Lookout Drive" in the early 1940's. Near the gazebo one would have found *View Point,* a stone cottage owned by the Barkofske family. It was the second of only two stone cottages on the lake at the time. Elsewhere on Lookout Drive was *Max Shack,* owned by the Virgil Pepperdine family and *The Bee Hive*, owned by W.A. and J.A. Shaw. The Shaw family actually kept bees in their attic. Another example on Look Out Drive, although the exact location is not certain, was *Vel-Joy-Joe* across from the beach house. That was the residence of the John Majempsey family.

A repurposed Girl Scout shelter house is now a year-round home at 29325 W. 153rd Terr (Lake Road 11) according to Larry Keegan, son of lake patrolman Philip Keegan, whose family used to reside there. According to Kenny Moll, the Boy Scouts had their club house at or near 29650 W. 152nd Street, on the hill overlooking the spillway. Interestingly, Lake Road 11 was referred to as "Scout Drive" in those early years. There you would find *Red Shutters,* the retreat of Mr. and Mrs. F.C. Wilson in the 1940s and 50s. Charla Wilson became a social reporter for The Gardner News and submitted long articles monthly keeping locals abreast of the news. Later abandoned for years, *Red Shutters* was demolished in early 2021.

Elsewhere, on Lake Road 11, in 1957, was *Bob-In*, the cottage belonging to Mr. and Mrs. Frank Mellusish. On the north end of the lake at that time, Mr. and Mrs. C.M. Bailey had *"Rocky Roost."* Though house numbers were introduced in Gardner in 1954, they were not yet assigned at Gardner Lake so exact locations are difficult to determine.

Today, on Lake Road 14, who hasn't noticed *Sanderosa?* This wonderful cottage on Pirate's Cove has been the joy of the Bob and Rosemary Sanders family for decades. The *Catfish Cabin* has now been restored at 29380 Lake Road 11. Aften McKinny's cottage near the gazebo at *Observation Point* on Lake Road 9 is appropriately named *Aften's Joy*. And how could we fail to mention the *Hodge Podge Lodge*, home of Jay and Jill Hodge at 15555 Lake Road 4.

Looking Back

On April 18, 1937, when the lottery tickets were drawn from a glass jar and lot locations were selected by ticket holders, Kansas City, Kansans George and Irene Rollheiser of Basehor hustled over to Lake Road 11 and staked out a lot near the point where the road intersected Lake Road 10. With the help of his brother, George built a fine stone and frame picnic pavilion, once very typical at the lake, which he completed in 1939. However, with the war raging in Europe, George felt compelled to join the Navy and put the little shelter on the market.

In August of 1941, Scottish immigrant John M. Rankin, who found his fortune in Kansas City land speculation, purchased the cottage with his wife Edith and deeded it over to their daughter and son-in-law, Mr. and Mrs. Hugh Stewart, as a gift in 1942. They added a septic system, and a bathroom. Eventually, the cottage was enclosed, enlarged and electrified and became a fine weekend retreat that remains today.

When Hugh and his wife passed, they left it to their only child, Charles "Chuck" Stewart, and it remained in that family for more than seven decades, qualifying the Steward family as a "First Family." Sadly, Chuck passed away in 2015, with no siblings or offspring, so the cabin left the family for the first time since 1941. But what survives today is a fully restored version of the 1939 cottage, which has been lovingly named "Catfish Cabin." It stands on its original site at 29380 Lake Road 11.

In 1939, John and Nettie Jeffries of Kansas City, Kansas, bought a lot on South Lake Road 5, or as it is also known, Gardner Place. During the 1950's, with the help of John's brother, Clifford, they built a modest cottage for weekend pleasure. Their daughter, Maxine Jeffries Stewart moved into cabin in 1971 and lavished it with the finishing touches. Sadly, she was only there for five years when she passed. However, in 1980, her daughter, Donna Stewart Wiliker moved in and went to work. She was aided by her roommate, Marilyn Hook, who like Donna, had grown kids who had left the nest. Unafraid to tackle any job, the two women sided the cabin with logs and installed four sliding glass doors for a commanding view of the lake, among other demanding tasks. It was during this time that Donna became the first and only Gardner Lake patrolwoman.

The First Families

In 1977, Donna's sister, Judy Scott, found a cabin on Lake Road 4, where she and her husband, Jon, settled in. Judy is still there today keeping the Jeffries' lineage alive on the sunrise side of the lake. When asked about her childhood memories, Judy relays the story of her father, Glenn Albert Stewart, teaching her, at the age five, how to bait a hook, remove the fish and clean it. She already had the fishing part down. It is one of her fondest memories as it made her feel so grown-up.

It is unknown how the Paul A. Speckin family came to own their lot at 15349 Lake Road 2, but they were here by October 1941. Their two kids, Rita and Paul Jr. spent many wonderful summers swimming and fishing at Gardner Lake. Lake Road 2 had one of the many parks that encircled the shoreline, so they were fortunate to have a stone picnic table and cook oven in their back yard. When Dorothy Otten married into the family in 1956, she too enjoyed the blessings of the lake. Although her husband, Paul Jr., has since passed, she retains her title as a Gardner Lake First Family. Their kids and grandkids enjoy it still.

The Reece Family at the Lake
Dr. A. S. Reece, the first physician for Transient Camp 9, also bought one of the original lots on Lake Road 12. Years later, he is seen here, the older gentleman on the right, with his family playing bridge on their porch overlooking the lake. (Photo courtesy of the Johnson County Museum)

Looking Back

In August of 1942, Ludwell Bryan, an electrical engineer from Kentucky, was relocated to Gardner to oversee and manage the conservation impact of the construction at the Olathe Naval Air Station. At the time, the Federal government was aware of the detrimental impact of earlier farming practices and wanted to proactively prevent a reoccurrence of another devasting dust bowl in the area. On his noon breaks, Ludwell went to Gardner to ask about farmland nearby that might be for sale. Through word of mouth, he heard that Art Bigelow was selling the remains of his farm that bordered the south shore of Gardner Lake. Ludwell and his wife Anna Beth purchased Bigelow's remaining 110 acres that was parceled for the project. This was the year that Ross, their first son, was born. Ross and his brother David have lived at the lake since.

In 1967, Ross caught wind that one of the original Gardner Lake Resort tourist cabins was slated for demolition. He jacked the cottage from its original block foundation at 15682 Lake Road 5 and planted it on his property at 16035 Gardner East Road. David has the home at the very southern point on the lake near the low-water bridge. When recently asked when he moved from the original homestead and to his current location at 16035 Gardner East Road, Ross quipped that, "I never have." His lake cottage is on part of the original family farmstead. Definitely, the Bryan family is a First Family.

The Stempski Family
Polish immigrant Walter Stempski, seated with hat, is shown here with his family at their stone cabin on Gardner East Road. He chose this lot to build for its gradual entry to the lake and the proximity of a beautiful park in their back yard. (Photo courtesy of the Delores Gribbin family archives)

The First Families

The Original Stempski Cottage
This stone cottage is still visible immediately north of 16068 Gardner East Road. (Photo courtesy of the Delores Gribbin family archives)

In 1946, Kansas City, Kansan, Walter Stempski, a Polish immigrant who became a railroad man, purchased three lots on Gardner East Road for $150 each. He and his wife, Marie, chose that location with his grandchildren in mind. It had a gentle, low entry to the lake, and a beautiful park to the south.

As a family project, they built a stone cottage on one of the lots. Stempski's granddaughter, Delores Friday Gribbin, recalls that they, as kids, were required to work in the mornings but then played all afternoon. In 1968, when the city of Gardner sold off property that included that park, Delores and her husband, with her parents, purchased three more lots through a bidding process. At one point, the family owned nine parcels. Delores still lives in the house at 16068 Gardner East Road that she and her husband built in the late 1960's. It's positioned to the south of the original cottage, which stands to this day. She made provisions for the property to stay in her family so that her grandchildren may enjoy it for years to come.

The Breitenstein clan is not only a First Family at Gardner Lake, but they must be the biggest. It all started in 1947 when John and Kate Breitenstein, and their nine kids, pitched in to buy a cottage on Lake Road 14. Unlike the

Looking Back

Cramer's situation, Kate was the driving force and the one with passion for the project. At the time, it was owned by Virgil and Marion Lemmon, who rented it to two Waves stationed at ONAS. The cottage is still there at 29395 W. 152nd Terrace. Its outward appearance has changed little, except for the three-exposure screened-in porch addition.

The Gardner News wrote about the Breitensteins in the summer of 1957. Evidently, patriarch John arranged for each son and daughter, with family of course, to spend a week at the cottage, with Sundays being open to all. According to the local paper, the family organized into a club that would hold twice-annual business meetings to discuss expenses. Each family

The Nucleolus of the Breitenstein Family
This 1945 photo shows Al and Kate Breitenstein with their adult children. In 1947, they purchased the cottage at 29535 W. 152nd Street on Pirate's Cove and set in motion what would be a family dynasty on Gardner Lake. (Photo courtesy of Jim Sanders family archives)

The First Families

member's commitment for upkeep at the time was four dollars paid a month at the time. The meetings were run by John, a banker by trade. At the spring meeting, they mapped out the calendar with family reservations. This was also the time to write, review and amend the rules and regulations, with no member exempt. The strictest rule was the Sunday availability to all. A mandatory-attendance spring cleaning was the big annual event.

In June 1957, newly-weds Robert and Rosemary Sanders, oldest grandson of Kate and John, honeymooned at the cabin. They eventually owned the cottage on the adjacent lot to the east, which remains in the family today. According to Tom, a third-generation Breitenstein, at one point, the family members occupied eleven cottages on the lake. If you have a neighbor named Sanders, Wyckoff, Locke, Collins, Sooter, Utz, Zignatio, Shindler or Humphrey, you are a neighbor of a Breitenstein.

Lake Road 4 resident Jim Sanders was one of thirty-eight grandchildren to spend his summer weekends on the north shore of Pirate's Cove. The family events were traditional German celebrations with dishes from the homeland served up with lots of brew. In the article he submitted that published in the *Kansas City Star Magazine* on August 3, 2008, Sanders said, "Many of us learned to swim, fish and sail at the lake." He went on to say, "But the greatest thing was getting to know my uncles, aunts and cousins to a degree that most families don't." The cousins' ages spanned thirty-two years. And by the time 2008 came around, those cousins had ninety-nine children, and an estimate of 200 grandchildren and growing.

Eventually, John and Kate Breitenstein's son, Walt, bought their parents' place and the remaining eight siblings bought lake cottages of their own, carrying on the family tradition. To date, there are four generations of Breitensteins at the lake, many of whom are year-round residents.

Chapter 17
FUN FACTS, FABLES AND LEGENDS

According to Jim Sanders, his cousin, Al Breitenstein, found a Ford Model T that had been submerged in the lake for years. He pulled it out, pounded out the pistons and rebuilt the engine. Al, Jim Sanders and his cousin, Bill Sanders enjoyed driving that car for years.

According to Brett Turnbull, there's a bomb shelter behind the Reed house at 29545 W. 152nd Terrace (Lake Rd 14). It was built in the 1950's by the occupant who, at the time, was a long-time employee of Bendix and had knowledge of ordnance. Incidentally, that house was originally a one-story structure until 1957, when a second level was added to accommodate the Reeds growing family. The Dan Reed family is also a First Family of Gardner Lake.

According to Dave Bryan, there was a time when people at the north end of the lake were having their houses burglarized. However, upon examination, the only missing items were potatoes. Later, a homeless man was found in the old latrine below the dam, living on the missing potatoes he cooked over a fire.

According to Dan Porter, the construction of his terrific, enclosed dock at 15425 Lake Road 3 was permitted only because the dock doubled as a fish hatchery. Inside the dock now is the bar and back bar from the Rendezvous Room at the old Muehlebach Hotel. Built in 1915, Rendezvous Room was the hang-out of Harry S. Truman and union boss Tom Pendergast, who certainly enjoyed their cocktails together at that bar.

Fun Facts, Fables and Legends

According to Glenn Bonar, whose family has lived on a local farm since 1928, there is a door to a Lockheed P2V "Neptune" in the bottom of the lake. The large patrol bomber, operated out of ONAS, jettisoned its door in preparation for the emergency ditch of the crippled bird. Bonar saw it tumble into the middle of the lake shortly before six parachutes appeared in the sky. The crew all survived. Not so for the plane, which ended up as wreckage in a nearby field.

In 1977 Frankie Moore's car was swept into the lake after he attempted to cross the south, low-water bridge during a storm. According to Richard McCreary, his headlights could be seen under water as the car drifted north with the current. This was confirmed by Ed Hayes, dive master and commander of the sheriff's office dive team at the time. In fall of 1985, then-GLA president, David Jackson, made the bridge improvement a top priority. With the cooperation of Johnson County, the construction began in 1987. Jackson's successful efforts brought the completion of the concrete bridge in 1988.

Ed Hayes recalls multiple incidences of occupied cars ending up in the lake on the north end at the dam and spillway. Mary Burnett reports that, on multiple occasions, she heard cars drive southbound into the lake at the curve by the fishing point on the east side. That curve now has a guard rail.

The Jackson Bridge replaced the low-water crossing, visible in the foreground, in 1988. The bridge was a top priority of then GLA president Dave Jackson beginning in fall of 1985.

Looking Back

According to Dave Jackson, past president of the Gardner Lake Association, both Ralph and Don Bray were eyewitnesses in 1932 to a police chase involving an escapee from Leavenworth Penitentiary. The high-speed event, which involved a dozen police cars, took the vehicles south on Gardner Road across the Kill Creek Bridge (under the mouth of Pirate's Cove before the lake was filled). It was a sight for two young boys to see, with guns protruding from all the windows. Richard McCreary, the boy's cousin, added that they told him that there was a guard strapped to the fender as a gunfire deterrent.

According to Karla Kuchemeister, whose family bought their cottage at 15847 S. Gardner Place in the 1950's, the lot immediately south of them held the clubhouse for the Hickory Grove Grade School's Cub Scout Troop. She distinctly remembers the structure before her family purchased the property and transformed the lot into a beautiful natural garden.

According to Ross Bryan, his former home at 16050 Gardner East Road was also moved here from Sunflower Ordnance Plant and was previously a duplex. An ad appeared in *The Gardner News* in July 1955, boasting of a liquidation sale at the Sunflower Village Housing Project. Duplexes sized twenty-one feet by fifty-two feet were available for $895, and duplexes sized twenty-one feet by forty-two feet were only $795. The ad goes on to say, "These houses have asbestos sheet siding, good roofs, oak floors and sheetrock interiors." And, "They can be moved anywhere near Sunflower, Kansas. A housemover will be on hand to quote moving prices."

According to Ed Hayes, former owner of the home at 15490 Lake Road 10, the brick veneer on the front of the house was reclaimed from the old Gardner railroad depot that was built in 1902 and demolished in 1983. The old depot was located on the west side of Center Street just north of the railroad tracks and immediately south of Gardner Disposal's currently location.

According to Glenn Bonar, the stone addition on the red house at 15650 Gardner West Road, adjacent to Lake Road 4, is built with tomb stones. And he should know, he helped with the construction in 1949.

Fun Facts, Fables and Legends

Aerial maps from the 1940s indicate that Lake Road 4 was the original Gardner Road built to circumnavigate the lake to the west. It ran uninterrupted all the way along the shoreline. Decades later, the road was straightened out in front of the golf course, with an abandoned section of that second road becoming Lake Road 4. Rumor has it that, sometime later, the cottage owner at 15555 Lake Road 4, had a load of dirt delivered in the night, and dumped in the middle of the old road to stop traffic from speeding by. That cottage now has a yard that extends to the new Gardner Road. It is the only Lake Road 4 house that does.

Fishing was serious business at the lake in the early years. The April 5, 1956, edition of *The Gardner News* announced the appointment, by city officials, of Mr. O. A. Homan as "Creel Census Clerk." Homan's job was to carry out the recommendations made by the University of Kansas after a biological survey of the lake in June 1955. An avid fisherman himself, Homan commenced to sinking one hundred tile and nail kegs in the lake for catfish nests. He lived at the first house north of the bathing beach, which still has a fireplace on the dock and an enclosed, built-in hatchery.

Through the decades at Gardner Lake, advocacy groups have sprung up among the residents for the care and improvement of the lake property. First, there was the Gardner Lake Corporation organized in 1933 to construct the lake. After completion, there was the Gardner Lake Lot Owners Association.

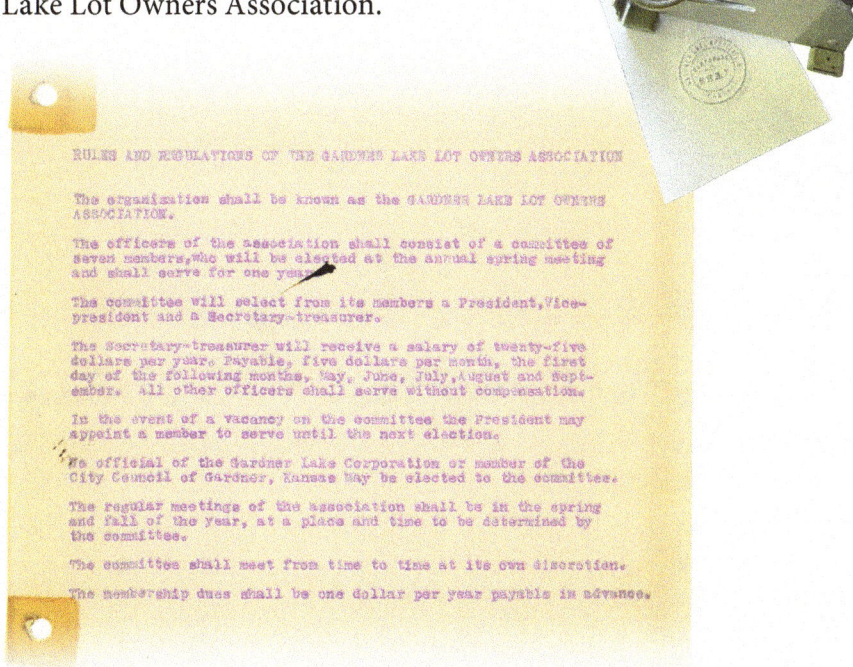

Looking Back

The Gardner Lake Breakfast Club was more of a coffee clutch. Then came the Gardner Lake Improvement Association. The longest surviving group, the Gardner Lake Association held its first meeting on August 11, 1957 and was incorporated in April 1960. In the July 23, 1960 edition of *The Gardner News*, they published this poem:

> *GLA is a new organization.*
> *News will appear for your information.*
> *It will be true and authentic too*
> *From this organization written for you.*
> *Some thinking people have banded together*
> *Inviting new things to join for the better.*
> *We've formed a council of nine members strong*
> *To act on measures to guide us along.*
> *A set of By-Laws to our great treasure*
> *Approved and adopted giving a measure*
> *Of right and wrong in daily living*
> *Around the lakes full protection giving.*
> *Already our strength is being felt.*
> *As we see distasteful things start to melt.*
> *There are wonderful people around the lake*
> *Good hearted, sincere, willing to give and take.*
> *There are many professions, just name'em-we dare*
> *They're here and we know they all do care.*
> *About the place where we work and play*
> *Knowing that rules were made to obey*
> *The Lake Patrolman and Councilman, KEN*
> *And City Officials together will win*
> *The goodwill of the Lake and of Gardner, too*
> *As they work with us in all that we do.*

Behind the Gardner Historical Museum's research center, The Bray House, at 207 W. Shawnee Street, sits a galvanized-metal, out-building that is serving as a garden shed. This is one of the last remaining structures associated with the lake construction. Evidently, according to an inventory of project structures, this was the booster pump house that served Transient Camp 9. It measures four feet by six feet and six feet tall and was previously mounted on stilts. Presumably, it served to fill the water tower at the center of the camp after it was treated at the filtration building, which is now 15787 Gardner

Fun Facts, Fables and Legends

Place. The structure was donated to the museum by long-time city resident Raymond Ayala and his daughter, Helen Wilson, after it had served for years as a shed behind their house at 309 Warren.

Is there really no Lake Road 13? There are plenty of references to Lake Road 14, now 152nd Terrace, that long stretch of road at the northeast entrance that runs from the spillway to the Bray Pond across from 15240 Gardner East Road. Then, there is the Lake Road 12 loop, but there is no reference to a Lake Road 13. Well, the Gardner Lake Corporation had such legendary bad luck, it is easy to see why they skipped that as a precaution.

In 2018, Rick Poppitz, reporter for *The Gardner News*, phoned in a scoop. A young woman committed suicide by hanging from the bridge at 159th and Gardner East Road. Upon hearing the entire story, the editor put their pencil down. They stated that the paper didn't report on suicides at the lake, and if they did, it would dominate the paper and would set a bad example, much less be depressing. There's just something about water. We go to water for peace. We came from water, we are mostly water, and we go home to water.

On the brighter side, we go to water for inspiration. We sing in the shower. Glenn Bonar proposed to his twenty-one-year-old girlfriend at the gazebo in 1960. Janet said yes, and they've been blessed since. There's just something about water.

Chapter 18

THE COVENANTS

History is history, like it or not. It is a sign of the times, as it should be. What follows is the transposition of the handwritten Gardner Lake Corporation covenant, filed into law on June 18, 1937. It contains restrictions that would be clearly unlawful now. Sadly, these restrictions were common during that period in U. S. history. The Gardner Lake Corporation dissolved on December 29, 1943. The restrictions survived the corporation but expired on June 18, 1962. The Civil Rights Act of 1964 would have made it a crime had it not expired on its own term. There was no attempt to renew them. There was a provision where residents could vote an expectation, or amendment to the restrictions, but no evidence of that occurring has been found.

Gardner Lake Lots

Being a subdivision of the following described tract of land in Johnson County, Kansas.

Descriptions:

A subdivision of Blocks 1, 2, 3, 4, 5, 6, 7, 8, 9, 10, 11, 12, 13, 14, 15, 16, 17, 18, 19 and 20 in the Gardner Lake Park as shows on this plat Details of Lots and Blocks locations shows on enlarged plats of said Blocks attached and made a part of this plat, Said Blocks being parts of the East ½ of Section of the west ½ of Section 12 and the northwest ¼ of Section 13, all in township 14 South Range of 22 East.

The Covenants

Restrictions on the following page.

The Gardner Lake Corporation, a corporation duly organized under the laws of the State of Kansas, proprietor of the above-described tracts of land has caused the same to be subdivided in the manner represented on this plot, which subdivision shall hereafter be known as GARDNER LAKE LOTS.

IN TESTIMONY WHEREOF The Gardner Lake Corporation has caused this instrument to be signed in its corporate name by its President and its corporate seal to be hereunto attized and attested by its secretary this 15th day of JUNE 1937.

Attest J. E. Johnson – Secretary

GARDNER LAKE CORPORATION

By R. J. Stockmyer, President

Restrictions

The use of the lots as designated on the accompanying plot are hereby made subject to the following restrictions and reservations which shall be deemed to be covenants running with the title to the land, and shall be binding up on the Grantees herein, and upon their heirs and assigns for a period of time hereinafter specified.

The property herein conveyed shall be used for private residence purposes only.

1. The plans of any residence or other buildings to be erected on said Lake Lots shall be approved by the Gardner Lake Corporation.

2. The property herein conveyed may neither be conveyed to, used, owned or occupied by negros or others of any but the white race.

3. No livestock or poultry shall be kept or maintained upon said Lake Lots.

4. Reservation is hereby made of the right to enter up on the rear ten feet of all lots therein and use the same for the erection and maintenance of poles and wires for telephone and electric lights and for the buildings and maintenance of water and gas pipes and the right of entry to repair and control same.

Looking Back

The forgoing restrictions and reservation shall be imposed upon each and every lot as per recorded plot thereof and the same shall continue in full force and effect for a period of twenty-five (25) years from June 15, 1937, and shall automatically be continued thereafter for succeeding periods of twenty-five (25) years each, provided, however that the owners in fee simple of the majority of the area of the lots in this subdivision. May release all of the lots hereby restricted from any one or more at the said restriction by executing and acknowledging an appropriate agreement or agreements in writing for such purpose and filing the same for record in the office of Register of Deeds for Johnson County, Kansas at least one year prior to the expiration of this first twenty-five (25) year period or any successive twenty-five (25) year period thereafter.

The balance sheet of the Gardner Lake Corporation 1934-1937.
This document was discovered in the basement of the Farmers Bank during their transition to the First Kansas Bank. It was slated for disposal but was rescued, with other archival documents, by Claude Steed who donated them to the Gardner Historical Museum. (Courtesy Gardner Historical Museum)

Epilogue
IT'S ALL IN THE CHASE!

The tone of this short chapter will be a little different. I am writing of a very personal experience that will require a 'first-person' tone to relate it properly.

I discovered the joy of historical research as a child. I must credit my father, Bud Heaven, with my innate curiosity for people and events of the past. Much to my mother's, Pat Heaven's chagrin, we invariably pulled over to every brown sign labeled 'historical marker' on our road trips so dad could read aloud to us. Those are among my most cherished memories.

Researching Gardner Lake history became on obsession for me several years ago. I want to relate a story of my navigation through the investigation of a homicide that occurred at the lake in the early 1950's. Maybe the reader will gain an appreciation of why someone would submerge themselves in a project at the expense of their professional career, their retirement savings, their health and certainly their housekeeping.

This all started with me in December 2019 when I was mining on Newspapers.com for subjects relating to the lake. This particular site did not have any Gardner or Olathe papers from my time frame, at that time, so I could only see syndicated reports picked up by other communities, or what might have appeared in the *Kansas City Times*.

This is where I stumbled upon the Leavenworth paper relating to a shooting at the lake on Friday, March 14, 1952. It had the ear-markings of a 'crime of passion' involving a thirty-year-old woman and two men in their late twenties. Evidently, one of the two men ended up dead in a summer cottage at the lake, shot five times from a .38 caliber handgun. Hardly an accident.

The names of the people involved where meaningless to me as the tenant lived at the lake as a renter. So, her name, Miss Ruby Thiry, was not familiar. I kept digging until I found an article that referenced the cabin owner as "Roark," also an unfamiliar name but at least I had something to work with.

I started reaching out to my 'brain trust' of native Gardnerites. My first call was to the retired captain of the Johnson County Sheriff's Department, Ed Hayes, who I knew lived on Lake Road 10 before he moved to Lake Road 4 in the early '70s. I was certain he could gain the court records or could steer me in the right direction. He was unfamiliar with the incident and never heard the name Roark, much less Ruby Thiry, but he would see what he could find out for me.

My next call was to my dear friend Richard McCreary, who had been championing me on this project. Roark…he knew the name! Reginald "Sheikh" Roark was a car dealer in the area with a dubious reputation. It was his wife, Helen, who, evidently, owned the cottage where she spent her summers. But Richard suggested that I call Kenny Moll, who knew everybody. There was that name again. I had been told by several people to call Kenny, and I hadn't found the occasion yet. But I dialed Kenny right away on that chilly December afternoon. The conversation went something like this:

> "Mr. Moll, my name is Amy Heaven and I'm writing a book about the history of Gardner Lake." Then, of course, I dropped Richard's name as they are good friends. I went on to say, "I'm researching a shooting that happened at the Roark cottage, would you happen to know where that was, by chance?" Kenny's response was, "Well, of course I do." Then he said, "I picked the woman up while she was walking in a

Kenny Moll with His Prized 1949 Ford
It was in this car that Kenny picked up Ruby Thiry during a March blizzard in 1952 after her involvement in a killing at a Lake Road 4 cottage. (Photo courtesy of Kenneth G. Moll family archives)

blizzard to the sheriff's office in Olathe to report that she'd shot her husband." Then he continued, "I drove her back to her cabin to use the phone."

Evidently, Kenny walked her to the door, gentleman that he is, and opened it to find a dead man lying on the floor in front of the couch. I had stumbled on a living witness who was overlooked entirely during the investigation that immediately followed that fateful event.

Looking Back

Needless to say, you could have knocked me over with a feather. But it gets better still:

> "Kenny, I'd love to get together with you and have you show me the cottage," I said. "What time is convenient for you, today?" I asked. Kenny's response was "Well, I'm really busy." Then he said, "I'll have to call you someday when my schedule gets clear…after the first of the year." My heart was pounding, and my head was throbbing. My prevailing thought was "You are 85 years old… how busy can you be!?!"

Yes, I realize that was very insensitive and selfish on my part. After all, I came across as some obsessed and crazy, old woman calling him out of the clear blue and demanding his time.

Of course, on January 2, I phoned Kenny to say "Happy New Year," then I baited him with a homemade shepherd's pie using ground sirloin from Steve's Meat Market in Desoto. He weakened slightly and agreed to meet me in a week.

After a sleepless night, I met Kenny on the morning of January 8. I found a sharp, attractive man who could have been in his late 60's or early 70's. I was so delighted to fill my notebook with his recollections and insights. I was having a grand time, and I think he was too!

Now, things come full circle. I asked him to please drive me to the scene of the crime. He drove slowly down Gardner Road then turned in front of a house on Lake Road 4. It was Ed Hayes' old house! The crime had occurred at Ed's cabin.

So, you can imagine how fascinating this has been for me. I respectfully called the current owner of the cottage, who wasn't wild about me going public with the address, so, of course, I won't. But I hope I have illustrated how much fun a person can have researching history or their genealogy. I hope everybody has something in their life of which they can find as much joy as I have.

Partial Index of Gardner Lake WPA Workers
THE GARDNER GAZETTE
And various other print media of the day

Ainsley, Anthony – (12/19/34 GG)

Anderson, Don "Juan" (7/4/35 *Spillway*)

Atwood, Cecil – "one of the camp boys" (4/28/37 GG)

Barrett, George – Electrician (12/26/34 GG), Super of Maintenance (2/6/35 GG), (3/13/35 GG)

Bellis, Roy – Left camp to work for JC McCreary (7/10/35 GG)

Bradford, Jas. R. – Asst. Camp Supervisor (7/10/35 GG)

Brannon, Joe – Editor, *Spillway* (7/4/35) (7/10/35 GG)

Breeden, Frank (12/26/34, 2/6/35)

Brisscoe, Jesse – (7/10/35 GG)

Brown, Alexander (1/9/35 GG) Possibly chef

Brown, Eugene – (2/20/35, 2/36/35)

Chesbro, Jack (Vernon Mayo Chesbro) – Camp Supt from Summer, 1934 to Sept, 1937

Chilen, H.D. (6/9/37) Landscape Architect on Project

Clary, Frank (12/11/34 GG)

Clary, John (12/11/34 GG)

Collins, John L., Chef (12/11/34, 3/6/35, 7/10/35, 2/26/35 GG)

Cordell, Neal 'Cot' – Truck Driver (1/2/35 GG), Foreman. Earth Moving Crew, Dam – (2/13/35, 7/10/35 GG)

Cordell, Stephen – (2/13/35 GG)

Dougherty, Mike – Assoc Editor, *Spillway*

Coughlin, Tom – (7/31/35 GG)
DeVoy, William (12/26/34, 3/6/35 GG)
Dotson, Fred – (7/10/35 GG) Artist, *Spillway*
Dougherty, Mike – (7/10/35 GG)
East, Tracy – Superintendent of Laundry (7/4/35 *Spillway*)
Eastland, Allen – (5/9/08 Gardner News)
Edenbo, John – 'Wood Surgeon', painter (12/11/34, 2/6/35, 2/13/35, 2/20/35 GG)
Emmons, Jesse – (7/10/35 GG)
Evans, Richard – (7/10/35 GG) Columnist (*Spillway*)
Farley, Bert – (3/13/35 GG)
Follis, David (3/13/35, 7/10/35 GG)
Glidden, H.K. – Resident Engineer (7/10/35 GG)
Griffing, Don – Dam Superintendent (6/36 GG)
Guthie (Guthey) Fred – Assistant Superintendent (11/28/34 GG)
Hall, Clinton – (7/10/35 GG)
Hesson, Aubrey – (7/10/35 GG)
Hicks, Lankie – (7/10/35 GG)
Johnson, "Singin'" Sam – (7/4/35 Spillway)
Jones, Shelby – Accountant, Secry to Superintendent, 2nd Superintendent – (2/20/35 GG), Camp Accountant (Summer, '36 GG)
Knisley, – (2/13/35)
Lopp, Roy – (3/13/35 GG)
Martin, Henry – (12/11/34 GG)
McCloud, John, Director of Recreation (3/6/35)
McCook, Sam – Assistant Case Taker (12/26/34, 2/13/35 GG)
McIsaac, Robert – Case Worker (7/10/35 GG)
McDowell, Walter (12/11/34 GG)
McQuage, Milton (7/10/35 GG)
McVoy, Charles (3/6/35)
Meisburger, R.G, – Case Worker (12/11/343, 12/26/34 GG)
Mohawk, Clifton – Seneca Indian (10/27/37 GG)
Montgomery, Oliver B. – Newspaper man (11/11/34 GG) Pharmacist, hospital orderly, recreational director (12/5/34 GG)

A gift to a friend.
Jack Chesbro was given this tramp art box as a parting gift by John Edenbo, presumably, the camp's "wood surgeon." It is in the style of the game boards and tables Edenbo made for the recreation center. It is now a family treasure of Linda Chesbro Wedman's.

Partial Index

Neison, Pump man. (7/10/35 GG)
Peer, Shine – (5/9/08 *Gardner News*)
Pfyne, Ray – (7/10/35 GG)
Phelps, Howard – (2/6/35, 2/13/35)
Posey, William – (3/6/35)
Prine, Ray – (1/9/35)
Ragan, J.L. – (7/10/35 GG)
Reece, A.S. – Doctor
Robinson, Ollie – (7//4/35 *Spillway*)
Russell, Clarence (1/9/35 GG)
Russell, Charles (2/6/35)
Rose, Roy, Chef – (2/20/35 GG)
Ryan, Joe – Seminole Indian (10/27/35 GG)
Schaeffer W. – Candy concession (1/9/35 GG)
Shaffer (Shafer), William (3/6/35, 2/13/35)
Shanholtz, W.G. – Stone Mason (various papers Jan, 1939)
Shaw, Walter (1/9/35 GG)
Shaw, Warren (7/10/35 GG)
Sherer, Harvey. Superintendent, Dam Construction (3/27/35 GG) (Jo Co Dem 8/8/35)
Smith, Harry (7/10/35 GG)
Soucy, Joe – Watchman (1 of the original 11 men) (7/10/35 GG) (7/4/35 *Spillway*)
Staten, Chester – Assistant Case Taker (12/26/34, 2/20/35 GG)
Swanson, Ed – (8/11/36 *Emporia Gazette*)
Sylvester, John – Secretary (11/28/34, 3/20/35 GG)
Tharp, George "Montana" – (3/20/35, 7/10/35 GG) Artist, *Spillway*
Thornburg, Clyde – Commissary Clerk, one of the original 11 (7/10/35 GG)
Till, – (3/20/35 GG)
Turley, Everett – (12/19/34 GG)
Wallace, Matthew – (7/10/35 GG)
Weeks, Max – Stenographer & Food Clerk (6/36 GG)
Wells, James – (7/10/35 GG)
White, Frank – (2/6/35)

Monument to a Friendship

Many Gardner Lake residents are not aware of a lovely green-spot adjacent to the Johnson County fairgrounds known as Cornerstone Park. There, under a protecting cover, hangs a substantial railroad bell. The origin of this small monument has deep ties to Gardner Lake history. Mica Marriott did some brilliant historic research on the subject and discovered its heritage and significance, which she shared in *The Gardner New*, September 18, 2009.

The back-story to this tribute started in 1934 during the depth of the Great Depression when the Kansas Emergency Relief Committee (KERC) adopted an effort to employ struggling artisans, craftsmen and laborers. Soon the Works Projects Administration (WPA) took over the project with Jack Chesbro as the Superintendent. Transient Camp No. 9 was established in the grassy area on the north end of Lake Road 5 where the footprint of the original mess hall and kitchen are still visible. As many as 244 men worked tirelessly for a few dollars a week, then returned to the camp in the evenings for a barracks lifestyle. They constructed our dam, spillway and the contributing stone structures such as the magnificent beach house, gazebo, well house, picnic pavilion, tables, ovens and latrines. In addition, they built six miles of roads with a fenced perimeter.

Joseph Jurovic was the electrician on the project. He and Chesbro struck up a friendship that transcended decades. In 1991, years after Chesbro's death in 1955, an elderly Jurovic traveled 800 miles from El Monte, California with the bell to commemorate their deep friendship. He placed it in Cornerstone Park, with a brass plaque, as a tribute to his friend.

Joe Jurovic
On his feet again, Jurovic poses for this photo after his service to Transient Camp 9 as electrician. He formed a friendship with camp Superintendent Jack Chesbro that lasted for decades. (Photo courtesy of the Gardner Historical Museum)

The bell itself was rescued by Jurovic from a Santa Fe Railroad steam engine destined for the scrap yard. After storing it for years, and declining many offers from organizations and collectors who wanted the historic bell, Jurovic decided to bring it home to Gardner where he had met and worked with Chesbro.

Further Dedication

This book is an offering to Herb and Helen Klemp, who gave so generously of their time and shared openly their family archives. Herb, being the world-class collector of all things, and especially scraps of paper, is perfectly paired with Helen, who is a tireless organizer of these things.

And to Kenny Moll, whose knowledge of this area is unsurpassed by anybody still living, with the possible exception of Tressa Stone. I relish the many hours I spent in one of Kenny's lawn chairs at his magical family farm on 151st Street, where the topic of the day was as diverse as the spectacular sunsets. Those hours are some of my most satisfying.

And to my dear friend, Tressa Stone. Tressa made the pursuit of my success on this project as much of an obsession as I have. To Tressa, it is impossible for me to adequately express my gratitude. We have formed a wonderful bond that will certainly survive this endeavor.

Tressa (Griffin) Stone with Cousin Shirley Smith
These girls are celebrating a birthday at the popular Lake Road 10 park in June 1952. Tressa eventually became the archivist who cataloged and preserved the Gardner Lake historical documents rescued by Claude Steed from the basement of the Farmers Bank Building. (Photo courtesy of the Tressa Griffin Stone family archives)

Acknowledgments

It's impossible for me to thank all the people and organizations that helped me on this endless project. But I will try here.

First of all, I thank Dave Young who came to accept my obsession with the lake's history, my frequent absenteeism in pursuit of research, the many associated distractions, and those blinky microwave leftovers.

Secondly, to my friends and colleagues at the Gardner Historical Museum who, not only opened their doors, but gave me a key so that I might do it at my convenience. Clearly, their archives regarding the lake were invaluable to this project. A special thank you goes to Claude Steed who is responsible for rescuing the original Gardner Lake Corporation documents from the basement of the old Farmers Bank building. Through his thoughtfulness and foresight, the documents were installed in the museum's archives for Tressa Stone to preserve and make available. Tressa then spent countless hours helping me link the lake history to that of the City of Gardner. Her knowledge of local history is extraordinary, and she is one of Gardner's hidden treasures.

I would be remiss if I didn't mention this partial, but ever-growing list of people and organizations to whom I am indebted:

Pete Adams, Sr.
Sandy Adams, Adams ProPhoto
Karen Barber
Glenn Bonar
The Breitenstein Family
Mary Gill Broski
Ross and David Bryan
Scott Burnett
Debbie Chappell
Debi Chavin
Teresa Coble, Kansas Historical Society
Cindy DeRosa
Charles Fruend
Mike Fruend
Gardner Lake Association
The Gardner Gazette
Gardner Historical Museum
The Gardner News
Oma Girsh
Delores Gribbin
Linda Hayden
Ed Hayes
Greg Hoots
Barbra Jacobe
Arnold Johnson
Johnson County AIMS
Johnson County Central Resource Library
Francie Locke
Johnson County Heritage Center
Kiesa Kay
Larry Keegan
Kenneth Spencer Research Library

Herb and Helen Klemp
Bob Kerr
Mica Marriott
Laura McCarthy
Richard McCreary
Laura Edemann McKaig
Kenny Moll
National Archives and Records Admin
Marg Leitner
Joyce O'Connor
Olathe Public Library
Mrs. John T. Patty
Irene Peer
Dan Porter
Cyndy Prier
Darlene Edemann Prier
Harold Quaintance
Brad and Nancee Rankin
Sharon Rose, City Clerk, Gardner
Judy Stewart Scott
Jim Shippee
Linda Sladdish
Anne Sooter
Charles Stewart
Robert Stockmyer
Claude Steed
Tressa Stone
Katie Reece Curry
Waubaunsee County Historical Society
Linda Chesbro Wedman
Donna Stewart Wiliker
Dave Young

Bibliography

"600 at Lake Opening: Gardner, Kas Fishermen Start at Sound of last." *The Kansas City Star.* May 15, 1940.

"A Big Day For Gardner: About 10,000 visit New Lake near Kansas Town." *The Gardner Gazette.* By The Star's Own Service. June 6, 1938

"A History of Gardner Masonic Lodge No. 65" Alex G. Powers. Powers Media. 2018

"A New Lake Open Today: Big Crowd of Fishermen Expected at Gardner, Kas." *The Kansas City Times.* May 15, 1940.

"A Raid Nets 100: Eight Persons Arrested by Johnson County Officials at Gardner Lake Party" *The Kansas City Star.* August 27, 1955.

"A Set-Back For Gardner Lake" *The Gardner Gazette.* March 7, 1934

"Accused of First-Degree Murder" *The Kansas City Times.* March 11, 1952

"Active at Laketown" – *The Gardner Gazette.* August 15, 1934.

Bickley, Walter – Phone interview with author. March 28, 2020.

Bigelow, Vi McConnell. Phone interview with author. December 27, 2019.

"Blaze Levels Gardner Lake Resort Building" *The Kansas City Star.* May 8, 1962

"Body Not Recovered From Gardner Lake" The Gardner News. June 12, 1952

"Body of Swimmer Found. Gary Boyd, 16, Drowned June 3 at Gardner Lake" *The Kansas City Times.* June 30, 1952

Bonar, Glenn – Phone interview with the author. February 18, 2022.

"Boy Swimmer Drowns: Friend Tells of Lake Tragedy Fatal to Gary Boyd, 16" *The Kansas City Times.* June 23, 1954

Breitenstein, Jack. Phone interview with author. October 16, 2019.

Breitenstein, Tom. Phone interview with author. April 1, 2020.

Bryan, Ross. Interview by author. Gardner, Kansas. January 21, 2017, October 15, 2019.

Burnett, Scott. Phone interview with author. April 18, 2022.

"Cabin Site Sales May Provide Lake" *The Gardner Gazette.* March 15, 1934

"Change at Lake Resort" *The Gardner News.* December 10, 1941.

Looking Back

Chesbro, Jack – "The Story of Camp Gardner." *The Gardner Gazette*. July 11, 1935.

Chesbro, Vernon – *Personal Memoir*. Unpublished.

Clark, Robert H. – "Heal A County Rift: Fatzer Is Assured of Accord Between Johnson Officials." *The Kansas City Times*. August 24, 1955

Close, Charles – *Conditions and Construction of Gardner Lake. Student Papers of Local History*. Johnson County Center for Local History, Johnson County Community College. 1986

Connelley, William E. – *History of Kansas State and People: Kansas At the First Quarter Post of the Twentieth Century*. The American Historical Society, Inc. 1928

Cramer, Frank – *The Home Town News of Gardner Kansas. 1942–1944*. Reprinted by The Gardner Historical Museum.

Fearon, Peter – *Kansas in the Great Depression: Work Relief, the Dole, and Rehabilitation*. University of Missouri Press. 2007

"Financing Of Lake Completed" – *The Gardner Gazette*. March 14, 1934

"Fire Destroys Lake Resort Building" – *The Gardner News*. May 5, 1952

"Fishing At Gardner Lake" – *The Gardner News*. April 12, 1956.

Fruend, Charles – Phone interview with the author. June 3, 2021.

"Full Speed Ahead In Gardner Lake Project." *The Gardner Gazette*. September 23, 1936

"Gardner Lake Camp." – *The Gardner Gazette*. June 10, 1936

Gardner Lake Corporation – A Collection of Official Correspondence. The Gardner Historical Museum.

"Gardner Lake Lost with Court Ruling." – *Olathe Mirror. March 8, 1934*

"Gardner Lake News: Highway Detoured Around Project Pending Re-routing." *The Gardner Gazette. June 9, 1937*

"Gardner Lake Site A Scene of Great Activity." *The Gardner Gazette*. May 27, 1936

"Gardner Now Has Its Own Water Plant." *The Gardner News*. March 5, 1959

"Gardner Proud of Lake: Fishermen Believe It Will Be An Anglers' Haven." *Kansas City Star.*
July 31, 1937

"Gardner Victim of Own Threat: Means of Stopping Water Belong to Navy, Captain Says." *The Kansas City Times*. April 9, 1965.

Gay, Roberta. Phone interview with author. November 29, 2019.

"Getting Ready for Beginning Work on Gardner Lake." *The Gardner Gazette. April 11, 1934.*

Girsch, Oma – "The Lake Meant More Thank Fishing to Gardner's Growth." *The Gardner News Progress Edition*. March 4, 1981

Gribbin, Dorothy – In person interview at Gardner Lake. September 9, 2021.

Hayden, Linda – Phone interview with author. August 8, 2020.

Bibliography

Hayes, Edward – Phone interview with the author. December 3, 2019.

"High Type of Men at Lake Camp: College Graduates Among Laborers on Project North of Gardner." June 23, 1937

"Honored by Two Nations for Valor." *The Kansas City Star.* June 17, 1962

Hootman, Lester. "Gardner Lake Association News." *The Gardner News.* August 23, 1962 – November 1, 1962

Hoots, Greg – *The Complete History of Lake Wabaunsee.* Blurb. 2008

"Huge Crowd Expected At Lake Next Wednesday: Day Marks Opening of Fishing Season." *The Gardner Gazette.* May 8, 1940

Jackson, David – "Gardner Lake to Celebrate Fiftieth Anniversary." *Kansas City Times* Centennial Edition March 18, 1987

Jackson, David – *History of Gardner Lake.* Gardner Lake Association Newsletter circa 2003.

Johnson, Arnold – Phone interview with author. August 6, 2020.

"Johnson County Fair Will Be At Gardner." *The Gardner Gazette.* January 17, 1920.

Johnson, Virginia Armstrong – *Where the Trails Divided.* Gardner Centennial Committee, 1957. Reprinted by The Gardner Historical Museum.

"Johnson County Fair May Come to Gardner." *The Gardner Gazette.* October 13, 1937.

Jurovic, John. Phone interview by author. April 22, 2017.

Jurovic, Joseph. *Letter to Oma Girsh.* July 17, 1990. Courtesy of Gardner Historical Museum.

Keegan, Larry. Interview by author. Gardner Lake, Kansas. June 11, 2019, April 14, 2020. June 21, 2021.

Kennedy, David H. – *Freedom of Fear: The American People in Depression and War 1929-1945.* Oxford University Press. 1999

"Lake Resort Sold." *The Gardner News.* February 19, 1959

"Laketown Soon To Become A Reality" *The Gardner Gazette.* May 30, 1934

"Lake Receives Coating of Oil from Fuel Tank." *The Gardner News* May 8, 1952

"Large Crowd was at Lake Sunday." *The Gardner Gazette.* May 12, 1937

"Machinery for Dam Construction is Here." *The Gardner Gazette.* March 27, 1935

"Map of Lake Project in this Issue: Names of Lot Owners Also Appear on Page Eight."
The Gardner Gazette. April 28, 1937.

Marriott, Mica – "The History and Folk Lore of Gardner Lake and Beach House." *The Gardner News.* May 9, 2008

Marriott, Mica. "Local Family's Memories of the Gardner Lake Beach House." *The Gardner News.* July 24, 2009.

Marriott, Mica – "Bell Serves as Reminder of Railroad's Importance in Community." *The Gardner News.* September 18, 2009

McCreary, Richard – In person interview with author. Gardner, Kansas. March 11, 2018

McIntire-Powell, Sadie – *Gardner Heritage*. Gardner Historical Museum. 1995

"Medal After 38 Years: British War Ministry Finally Locates A Veteran." *The Kansas City Star*. January 19, 1939

Moll, Kenneth G. – In person interview. January 8, 2020.

"News About Gardner Lake." *The Gardner Gazette*. March 28, 1934

"New Management at Gardner Lake Club." *The Gardner News*. March 29, 1956

"New State Lake at Gardner Assured." *Johnson County Democrat*. February 8, 1934.

Nichols, John H. *Gardner Lake. A WPA Project*. 1996 – Unpublished Research Paper.

Patty, Frances – *Gardner Lake News*. A collection of social articles for *The Gardner Gazette*. 1942-1944.

"Plan Gardner Lake Fete: Completion of the Project to Be Marked Sunday." *The Kansas City Star*. April 14, 1937

Pritchard, Mary. Phone interview with the author. December 2, 2019.

"Prospects for Lake Brighten." *The Gardner Gazette*. March 7, 1934

"Prospects Point to Continuation of Work on Gardner Lake." *The Gardner Gazette*. December 11, 1935.

Rattenne, Dorothy "Dot." Phone interview with author. March 24, 2020.

Reece, A.S. *Socialized Medicine at the Grass Roots*. Gardner Historical Museum. Copyright 1977

Relief, Recovery and Reform: The New Deal in Johnson County. Album Volume XIV Number 1, Winter 2006. The Johnson County Museum.

"Repair Work On Gardner Spillway." *The Kansas City Star*. June 28, 1962

"Resume of Progress of WPA in Past Year: Figures Are Released concerning Activities of Organization." The Gardner Gazette January 1, 1941

Ruiz, Richard "Poncho." Phone interview with author. February 10, 2022.

Sanders, Jim. "Our Family Place on Gardner Lake.' *Kansas City Star Magazine*. August 3, 1984

"Saving The Trees." *The Gardner Gazette*. November 3, 1937.

Scott, Judy Stewart. Phone interview with author. April 18, 2022.

Seals, Ross. In person interview with author. Olathe, Kansas July 17, 2020.

Shlaes, Amity. *The Forgotten Man*. Harper Collins, NY 2007

Smith, Jean Edward – *FDR*. Random House Trade May. 2008

"Some Random Facts and Thoughts About the Proposed Gardner Lake." *The Gardner Gazette*. February 14, 1934

Sooter, Anne Breitenstein. Phone interview with the author. January 21, 2017.

Speckin, Dorothy. Phone interview with the author. June 25, 2021.

"Start Work on Lake Site Camp." *The Gardner Gazette*. June 6, 1934.

BIBLIOGRAPHY

"State Lake Camp News." *The Gardner Gazette*. August 22, 1934

"State Lake Camp News." *The Gardner Gazette*. February 20, 1936

"State Lake for Gardner Seems Almost a Certainty." *The Gardner Gazette*. February 7, 1934

"State Lake for Gardner Assured." *The Gardner Gazette*. February 21, 1934.

"Stop Work on Lakes: Gardner and Wabaunsee Projects at Standstill." *The Kansas City Star.* January 23, 1936.

"Suit Against Sheriff Williams: Former Operator of Resort Alleges He Was Struck." *The Kansas City Times*. August 15, 1958.

"Thanks to These Men." *The Gardner Gazette*. December 5, 1934

"The Friendly Star." *The Gardner Gazette*, June 14, 1939

"The Kansas Emergency Relief Committee." *Press Release #135*. October 3, 1933. The Kenneth Spencer Research Library. Lawrence, Kansas.

"The Kansas Emergency Relief Committee." *Press Release #147*. January 23, 1936. The Kenneth Spencer Research Library, Lawrence, Kansas.

"To Celebrate Fourth at Lake Camp." *The Gardner Gazette*. June 26, 1935

"Transient Workers Camp to be Opened with Housewarming." *The Gardner Gazette*. October 10, 1934.

"Two Held on Murder Charge: Man and Woman Accused in Shooting at Gardner Lake."
The Gardner News. March 13, 1952.

United States Department of the Interior – National Register of Historic Places Registration Form: WPA Beach House At Gardner Lake. Prepared by Martha Hagedorn-Krass, Architectural Historian. April 21, 1992

Uys, Errol Lincoln – *Riding the Rails: Teenagers on the Move During the Great Depression.* T.E. Winters and Sons. 2014

The Spillway. The Most Home Like Transient Camp. Vol -1, Number 1. Unofficial Publication of the Kansas Emergency Relief Committee. July, 1935. Kenneth Spencer Research Library, Lawrence, Kansas

"Water Issue Boils as Mayor Vs. Navy." *The Parsons News*. April 8, 1965

"Water Tops Spillway At Gardner Lake: Maximum Level Attained Last Saturday Evening. Throng Present Sunday." *The Gardner Gazette*. May 18, 1940

Wedman, Linda. Interview by the Author. Lawrence, Kansas. April 30, 2017, and March 30, 2019

"Wife of Co-Defendant: Marriage is Revealed by Olathe Cape Operator." *The Kansas City Times* March 13, 1952.

Wiliker, Donna Stewart. Phone interview with the author. April 18, 2022.

Wiley, George. "Gardner Lake Association News." *The Gardner News*. July 17, 1959 – May 24, 1962

"Will Change Lake Resort To Skating Rink." *The Gardner News*. 2-12-59

Looking Back

Wilson, Charla Hudler – "Gardner Lake Happenings." *The Gardner News*. Social column December 13, 1956 – August 13, 1959.

Wolfe, Carol – "Gardner, Kansas: A Demographic Study 1857-1925, A Personal View 1920-1984." Unpublished Manuscript.

"Work Halted On Lakes." *The Emporia Gazette*. January 23, 1936.

"Workers' Camp Will Require More Than Six Carloads of Lumber." *The Gardner Gazette*. May 16, 1934.

Worster, Donald. *The Dust Bowl: The Southern Plains in the 1930s*. OUP 2004

Whyte, Kenneth. *Hoover: An Extraordinary Life in Extraordinary Times*. Random House Audio

INDEX

A

Pete Adams Sr. 78
Alexander, E. F. 8, 11, 12, 14, 16, 19, 40, 54, 56
Alexander, Lillian 11
Alexander, Mac 11
Alexander the Goose 79
Allenbrand, Smitty 97
Armstrong, Eldon E. 19
Aver, Paul R. 100
Ayala, Raymond 137

B

Baird, Jess 92, 95
Barber, Karen 111
Bernhardt, J. R. 85
Bickley, Walt 101
Bigelow, Art 20, 128
Bigelow, Howard C. 14, 20, 42
Black, Lucy Cristler 42
Bonar, Glenn 50, 75, 97, 107, 133, 135, 137, 152
Bonar, Janet 137
Bonds, Bill 79
Bray, Don xi, 78, 133
Bray, Ralph xi, 133
Breitenstein, Al 77, 132
Breitenstein, John 129, 130, 131
Breitenstein, Kate 129, 130, 131
Breitenstein, Tom 131
Breitenstein, Walt 131
Brown, Mr. and Mrs. 87
Bryan, Anna Beth 128
Bryan, David 152
Bryan, Ludwell 128
Bryan, Ross 97, 134
Burnett, Mary 133
Burnett, Scott 103, 152
Burton, Joe 100

C

Campanella, Denise Churchwell 102
Campbell, M. R. 15
Chesbro, Fernie Sowers 27
Chesbro, Jack 27
Chesbro, Vernon M. "Jack" 24, 25
Chesbro, Vernon "Sonny" 24, 27
Churchill, Winston 59
Churchman, Nellie 95
Churchman, W. R. 95
Combs, Lula Long 59
Cook, Mrs. 87
Cordell, J. S. 66
Cordell, Neil "Cott" 88
Cramer, Charles 66
Cramer, Frank 9, 109, 111
Cravens, Clifford C. 88, 112
Cristler, George W. 42
Cristler, Mike 42, 43
Cristler, P. V. "Tiny" 42

D

Daggs, Rolla 101, 102

E

East, Tracy 37
Edemann, Thomas Jefferson "Jeff" 98
Edenbo, James 25

Eskridge, Kansas 23, 25, 52
Ewing, U. F. 68
Eyerly, Harry 54
Eyerly, Mrs. Earl 28

F

Farmers State Bank 10, 16
Federal Emergency Relief Agency 21
First Presbyterian Church 32
Fleming, W.D. 15
Flint, Lazarus 5
Freund, Charlie 97, 100
Freund, Linda 100
Freund, Mike 100

G

Gardner Lake Association viii, ix, x, xii, 22, 29, 49, 53, 54, 55, 73, 79, 80, 123, 133, 135, 152, 155, 157
Gardner Lake Breakfast Club 135
Gardner Lake Corporation iii, v, 14, 15, 16, 17, 19, 20, 21, 42, 48, 72, 124, 135, 137, 138, 139, 151, 154
Gardner Lake Improvement Association 67, 135
Gardner Lake Lot Owners Association 66, 110, 135
Gay, Jody 78
Gay, Roberta 78, 154
Gene Gay 78
Girsh, Oma 152, 155
Grahovac, Paul 70
Gribbin, Delores Friday 129
Griffing, Don 58

H

Harrington, Martin 12, 47
Hayes, Ed 71, 101, 133, 134, 142, 144
Hayes, James Y. 97
Haynes, L. C. 15
Heaven, Bud iii, 141
Heaven, Pat iii, 141
Higgins 108
Higgins, Herman 66
Hook, Marilyn 126
Hoover, Herbert 5

Horman, O. A. 135

J

Jackson, Dave xii, 133
Jacoby, Barbra 79
Jeffries, Clifford 126
Jeffries, John 126
Jeffries, Nettie 126
Jerovic, Joe 25
Johnson County Sheriff's Department 71
Johnson, J. E. 139
Johnson, Virginia Armstorng 12
Johnson, Virginia Armstrong 155
John Stutz 28
Jones, Shelby 52, 56, 58, 88, 116

K

Kansas Emergency Relief Committee 11, 15, 21, 22, 25, 28, 37, 39, 42, 148, 157
Kansas Forestry Fish and Game Commission 48
Kansas State Historical Preservation Office 79
Kansas State Historical Society 79
Kaserman, F. A. 48
Keegan, Larry 78, 101, 102, 125, 152
Keegan, Phil 83, 102
Klemp, Brenda 123
Klemp, Heinrich "Heinie" 71, 122, 123
Klemp, Helen Grove 65, 71, 75, 108, 122, 123, 149, 152
Klemp, Herb 65, 71, 75, 108, 119, 122, 123, 149, 152
Klemp, Kathryn 123
Klemp, Melissa 123
Klemp, Wilhelmina "Mimi" 71, 122, 123
Krough, Lyle 97
Kuchemeister, Karla 98, 134

L

Lake Wabaunsee 25, 27, 52, 155
Langdon, Alf 40

Index

Leitner, Marg 79
Lemmon, Marion 130
Lemmon, Virgil 130
Lyon, Frank B. 17, 18

M

Manning, James Jr. "Jim" 69
Manning, James Sr. "Jimmy" 69
Marriott, Mica 148, 152
Mathes, Bert 89
Mathes, Marion 'Mike' L. 89
McCreary, C. S. 66
McCreary, Florence Bray 47
McCreary, James 47
McCreary, Richard 11, 47, 78, 133, 142, 152, 156
McDaniels, Paul 100
McGrath, John 23
McIntire-Powell, Sadie 13, 50
McKaig, Laura Edemann 99, 152
Michaels, Ray R. 110
Miller, L. A. 69
Miller, L. A. Sr. 69
Miller, Mr. and Mrs. Ray 95, 96
Modic, John 111
Moll, Kenny 50, 89, 97, 125, 142, 143, 149, 152
Moore, Frankie 133
Moore, Shelby 104

N

National Register of Historic Places 79, 157
Newall, Wayne 86
Nichols, John 31
Noble, W. V. "Scotty" 92, 95

O

Olathe Lake 113

P

Patty, Frances (Mrs. John T.) 62, 109, 111, 152, 156
Payne, Howard E. 15
Peer, Irene Eastland v, 35, 96
Pendergast, Tom 132
Poppitz, Rick 137
Porter, Dan 132
Powers, Alex G. 18, 36, 153
Price, G. F. 28
Prier, Darlene Edemann 99, 152
Prier, Gary 99
Pritchard, Mary 96

R

Rankin, Edith 126
Rankin, John M. 126
Ranney, Guy 88
Rattenne, Dorothy "Dot" 78, 156
Rattenne, Mike 78
Rattenne, Mike Jr. 78
Rattenne, Mitzi 78
Rattenne, Tammy 78
Reece, A. S. 11, 66, 104, 127
Reed, Dan 132
Reese, Mr. and Mrs. Ebb 87
Reese, Ralph 87
Roark, Helen 142
Roark, Reginald "Sheikh" 142
Roesser, Tom 83
Rollheiser, George 126
Rollheiser, Irene 126
Roosevelt, Franklin D. 10
Ruiz, Poncho 101

S

Sanders, Bill 132
Sanders, Jim 130, 131, 132
Sanders, Robert 125
Sanders, Rosemary 125
Santa Fe Trail 4
Schmutz, L. R. 74
Scott, Jon 127
Scott, Judy Stewart 127
Scott, Karen Rohner 123
Shanholtz, Willis G. 59, 60, 147
Shannon, Mike 56
Shriver, E. E. 15
Sladish, Linda 102
Smith, Ruby 95
Speckin, Dorothy Otten 156

Speckin, Paul A. 62, 127
Speckin, Paul A. Jr. 127
Speckin, Rita 127
Steed, Claude 56, 150, 151, 152
Stempski, Marie 129
Stempski, Walter 70, 128, 129
Stewart, Charles "Chuck" 126
Stewart, Glenn Albert 127
Stewart, Maxine Jeffries 126
Stewart, Mr. and Mrs. Hugh 126
Stockmyer, Bob 101, 103
Stockmyer, Jean 16
Stockmyer, Joan 16, 48
Stockmyer, John 16
Stockmyer, Minnie 16, 48
Stockmyer, R. J. 14, 15, 16, 24, 28, 31, 139
Stockmyer, Robert Kirkland "R. K." 15, 16, 19, 24, 31, 66
Stutz, John 28, 37

T

Thiry, Ruby 142, 143
Truman, Harry S. 132

Turkeyfoot, James 5
Turnbull, Brett 132
Turner, Ollie 15

V

VanArsdale, Shirley Bruce Brown 96
Volz, Bertha 122, 123
Volz, Phillip 122, 123

W

Westhoff 78
Westhoff, Clyde 78
Westhoff, Jim 76
Westhoff, Susan 78
Westminster Hall v, 9, 32
Whitlia, J. R. 15
Wiliker, Donna Stewart 103, 126, 152
Wilson, Charla 117, 120, 125, 158
Wilson, Helen Ayal 137
Winkler, H. C. 109
Winters, Gary 78

Art Credits

Page xii – Brenda and Melissa Klemp with Ross Amyx, 1975.
Photo courtesy of the Herb and Helen Klemp family archives.

Page 3 – Jean Zuk being charmed by Herbie Klemp, 1956.
Photo courtesy of the Herb and Helen Klemp family archives.

Page 26 – Friends gather on the Klemp dock, Lake Road 8, 1956.
Photo courtesy of the Herb and Helen Klemp family archives.

Page 47 – View looking towards the northwest corner of the dam as the lake starts to fill in 1937.
Photo courtesy of the Charles Rogers collection, Gardner Historical Museum.

Page 63 – Brenda and Melissa Klemp feeding the ducks. 1969.
Photo courtesy of the Herb and Helen Klemp family archives.

Page 83 – Mimi Klemp taking a sunbath, July, 1948.
Photo courtesy of the Herb and Helen Klemp family archives.

Page 137 – A diving lesson for Herbie Klemp, July, 1946.
Photo courtesy of the Herb and Helen Klemp family archives.

About the Author

Amy Heaven is a career general aviation aircraft broker and aviator with a passion for American history and historic preservation. A native of Lake Quivira, Kansas, she returned to live in Gardner after a twenty-year stint in Lexington, Missouri where she spearheaded multiple architectural preservation projects that received state recognition. A tireless volunteer, she served the Lexington City Council, The Lexington Preservation Commission, the Lexington Tourism Commission as well as the Lexington Historical Association.

While renovating a tear-down home on Gardner Lake in 2011, she became captivated by the history of the construction of the lake. Her attempt to research the details of the project for pleasure, brought about an awareness that little had been written about the epic event that occurred during The Great American Depression. The unwritten manuscript became a bucket-list item with research beginning in 2014. Not a stranger to writing having authored numerous trade magazine and newspaper articles, *Looking Back* is her first book.

www.ingramcontent.com/pod-product-compliance
Lightning Source LLC
Chambersburg PA
CBHW061406010526
44119CB00011B/276